Own Your Sh*t: You're The Problem

Look in the Mirror

No One Else Is Coming to Save You

Nick Groves

Published by Nicholas Groves, Columbus, Ohio

Cover design by Najdan Mancic

Edited by Shannan Zerance

Printed in the United States of America

Dedication

To my amazing and beautiful wife, Rachel. You never let me bullshit myself. This book exists because I am determined to become the kind of man you deserve.

Disclaimer

The examples in this book come from a lifetime of mistakes, lessons, and observations. Some are mine, some are pulled from the world around me, and a few of them are direct callouts to specific people, jobs, or situations. I didn't write this to gossip; I wrote it to punch holes in the bullshit we all hide behind.

If you happen to see yourself in one of these examples and get offended, let me save you the trouble, that's not on me. That's your guilt talking. I don't owe you protection from your own reflection. If the shoe fits and it pisses you off, then wear the damn shoe and walk through the rest of this book anyway.

I'm not here to sugarcoat or babysit. If you're looking for a soft landing, you bought the wrong book. If you're ready to stop bullshitting yourself, you're exactly where you need to be.

If you can't handle this, close the book now and go read something else.

Additionally, every effort has been made to ensure accurate information and references at the time of publication. However, I cannot accept responsibility for changes that occur after publication. I have no control over and do not assume responsibility for the content of any third-party websites or sources mentioned.

Contents

Intro

Let's just get this out of the way right now: You're the problem.

Not your boss.

Not your schedule.

Not your genetics, your parents, your friends, your childhood, or your so-called "bad luck."

You.

If that stings, good. It's supposed to. This book isn't here to pat your back or sprinkle sugar on the truth. It's here to hold up a mirror and make you face the one person screwing up your life the most—you.

You want a better body? Earn it. Eat less, move more.

You want more money? Stop wasting it. Work harder, work smarter.

You want more respect? Act like someone worth respecting. Less talking, more doing.

The truth is that simple, radical self-responsibility and accountability are the only ways anything changes.

Nobody's coming to save you. Nobody's going to walk into your life and suddenly fix your mess. If you don't do it, no one will. And while you're busy waiting for things to "get better," someone else out there is already doing the work you keep avoiding.

If that feels harsh, it's because it is.

Chances are, you might be the problematic friend or family member. You might be the person at work who thinks they're doing a good job, but in reality, nobody can stand you, and they want you to quit because you're toxic.

If it feels unfair, good; life doesn't owe you fair. It only responds to effort.

So think about it. Right now. Do you have the life you want? The job, the body, the friends, the respect, the confidence? Or are you tired, broke, pissed off, and wondering how the hell you ended up here again?

Maybe you're burnt out. Maybe you're barely hanging on. Maybe you've hit that point where you start thinking the world would just be better off without you. I've been there. I know what that hole feels like. It's cold, it's quiet, and it makes you believe the lie that this is all you'll ever be.

I'm not some motivational guru or millionaire with a perfect morning routine. I'm a 32-year-old, still-in-an-apartment, mid-career, nobody who got tired of listening to his own bullshit.

This book isn't here to make you feel better, it's here to make you better. It's a punch in the mouth followed by a hand up. A mirror, not a manual. You want to change your life? It starts right here, with you owning your sh*t.

Get the fuck up. We've got work to do

PART 1:
THE MIRROR

We All Eat, Sleep, & Fuck Things Up

There I was, in the bathroom, going toe-to-toe with a particularly nasty flu, when I felt a pang.

My heart kicked. Then again. Then a third time, but weaker.

Each one after felt more half-assed than the one before, as if my heart was checking out.

My head swam, a bout of anxiety surged, and the room was on fire.

Was this really how I was about to go out? Not even 29 years old, 325 pounds, mid-shit?

Seconds that felt like minutes passed before clarity and ease returned. Gathering my senses, I thought to myself. *What the fuck am I doing?*

Only a year out of blue-collar work, I had put on a ton of weight now that I was at a desk every day. Mountain Dews daily, shit food, no exercise, a car that barely ran, spending money just as fast as it was coming in. I was a ticking time bomb.

It's not that I was all-out lazy and rotting life away. I was just consistently choosing comfort over everything else. Career wasn't going terribly; it's actually where I was putting the most effort in. But that would mean nothing if I croaked right here.

It was time that I got my fucking shit together.

I had "dieted" many other times, but nothing ever stuck. Not because they were bad diets, but because I'd use every excuse to avoid them, and I knew it.

This time was different. I did the research, set my daily calorie max, and refused to budge. I had no idea that this course of action would lead me down a path of self-improvement that would change my life forever.

After two months, I was down 20 pounds from dieting alone. No exercise. I was on YouTube when I stumbled upon a video titled something like "My Time on 75Hard." Curious, I checked it out.

I learned about a 75-day mental toughness challenge that seemed nearly impossible at the time. I was immediately hooked. It seemed like the kind of thing I was in a rhythm to pick up. Something challenging that would push my limits. Every day, you had to follow the same rules, and if you failed even a single one, you had to restart back at day one.

Things, for example, like two separate workouts every day, drinking a gallon of water, and sticking to a diet with absolutely no cheat meals.

It was by far the hardest thing I had ever done for myself. It took 85 days to complete because I had to restart on day 10 after learning the "no additives" part of the gallon of water rule.

Over those 85 days, I lost another 35 pounds and gained a significant amount of muscle. I had also learned a great deal about myself, my goals, my capabilities, boundaries, and excuses.

My career also saw an immediate upturn due to the mentality changes I was experiencing. In the year I did the Live Hard program, I would need two hands to count the number of amazing things that came my way from promotions, pay changes, travel opportunities, and all-around respect and trust I earned.

But by now, you're probably wondering how you and I relate.

Look, I'm an everyday dude. There's nothing different between you and me. I get up and go to work so that I can afford the lifestyle I want. I have my wins, and I have my losses. I stress sometimes, and I thrive other times. I'm just a regular guy who grew up middle-class, then made enough poor choices to land myself on bad days where I had to choose whether to feed myself or my cats. I'm a guy who's chosen to learn every lesson at the bottom of life's boot while it kicked me in the mouth.

Like you, I'm good at some things, and I fucking suck at others.

And I'm not speaking from the clouds, either. I don't sit here and write to you from the study of some house I own while my butler massages my feet. No, I sit here in my two-bedroom apartment with a space heater and a blanket, thinking about finances because my dog decided to tear another ACL last week.

However, I have experienced a boon in my life over the past couple of years: some stresses gone, some respects gained, and being able to afford my dream car, a Jeep Wrangler. Life is moving rapidly, my career is growing steadily, and my mindset is sharpening daily.

Every positive thing I've seen has been a result of my own hard work.

Every negative thing? A result of my lack of accountability.

I no longer wonder why I went through so many years of shit when I was perfectly capable of doing better. Why was I broke, fatter, and going nowhere in life?

If I had to choose one lesson to teach the world from my ever-growing list of life lessons, I would easily narrow it down to a single thing.

YOU are the fucking problem.

Why Does It Matter?

Responsibility or accountability. Which one are we talking about, and which one is more important? Well, both. They go hand-in-hand with each other, and you need both to not be a shit stain in society, your place of work, or your relationships.

You're probably asking, 'What's the difference?' I'll save you the trouble of Googling it yourself.

Self-responsibility is the expectation that you have to do certain things or act in certain ways.

Self-accountability is taking ownership of your actions or behaviors regardless of the outcome.

While you can't always control what you're responsible for, since we are all part of the same planet and communities, you can take control of your actions and how their outcomes are handled.

Responsibility: You're supposed to maintain your health and do what is necessary to maintain your well-being.

Good Accountability: You generally eat a clean diet and exercise enough to maintain your health. You also wash your hands regularly when out in public and take care to avoid others who are obviously unwell.

Good Outcome: You live a longer and more comfortable life because your body is well taken care of. You get to involve yourself in nearly every activity you want because you maintained your health in the things you could knowingly control. And because you took care to avoid sickness, you are known to be more reliable in being present at work and for your friends and family than if you were not.

Poor Accountability: You prioritize comfort, time, or the flavor of your favorite ice cream over all else. Now you're tubby, can't tie your shoes, and are headed for a heart problem faster than you can scarf down a pizza. Additionally, you've got a cold every other week because you've never bought a bottle of hand sanitizer in your life. But none of this is your fault; you've heard that some people have a poor metabolism, so that must be it.

Poor Outcome: Because you didn't put in the effort to control the controllable (you), you're now forced to miss out on things because you're physically unable to participate. You're now paying for extra seats on an airplane, and your health insurance costs are higher. Not to mention your friends or boss are now used to you not showing up because you're "sick" again. Worse, your loved ones may have to adjust their lives to take care of you because you didn't. Or at the end of the spectrum, you're fucking dead.

And this is all just physical. Think about the mental benefits and consequences you'll experience from this as well. The growth, happiness, or elation versus the depression, anxiety, or blame. Throughout this book, I'll provide many more examples of how our actions or lack thereof cause our wins and losses. Additionally, you'll find a section in the back of each chapter where I list more real-world examples of Excuses vs. Truths.

This book isn't a manual or another step-by-step plan. It's a mirror pointing right back at you. Calling out and using real-life examples of piss-poor attitudes and behaviors in the hopes that you find something that makes you think, "Oh, shit, I've said or done that." Or "Wait, I know someone like that."

Once it's in your head enough, or you start recognizing these examples in public, they'll be easier to relate to yourself. We're wired to judge people; it's built into us. But here's the trick: don't use it as a weapon, use it as the mirror.

When you catch your neighbor being lazy, your friend lying to themselves, or your coworker making excuses, don't roll your eyes like you're better than them. Chances are, you're doing the same things in quieter ways. Use their examples to call yourself out.

When you stop judging for ego and start observing for awareness, you'll notice it gets a hell of a lot harder to lie to yourself. None of us has superiority over others; we're all assholes living on the same planet. So don't think you're a better asshole than the one next to you.

But here's where this really matters: accountability doesn't stop with you. You live in society. Whether you like it or not, your behavior affects those around you. When you stop taking responsibility for yourself, it bleeds onto the rest of us. Your laziness becomes someone else's problem. Your indifference becomes someone else's mess to clean up.

There's a dog park near my neighborhood with a double-gate system set up on each side, each meant to keep the dogs safe from bolting into traffic. These gates are far apart, and you can't really see one from the other. Every damn week, I'll drive by and see that both gates on one side are left wide open. Someone must stroll out, phone in hand, utterly detached from the fact that someone else's dog could be let in from the far side and sprint through, straight into the street.

That's what the absence of accountability looks like. It's not always someone robbing a bank or cheating on their taxes or putting themselves in hardships. So often it's tiny, thoughtless moments, people too wrapped up in their own world to think, "Hey, I should close that gate for the next person." That's all accountability really is, decency with follow-through.

This is why it fucking matters. Because when enough people stop taking ownership, society stops working. Every lazy moment compounds. Every "not my problem" turns into someone else's tragedy. Accountability is what holds the line between civilization and chaos. It's what separates people who give a damn from people who just exist.

How You Drive Is How You Live

For a few years, I've been developing this theory or belief that you can tell so much, if not nearly everything, about a person's level of accountability, responsibility, and ego by how they use their car in a place around other drivers and pedestrians. In short, you can tell just how much of an asshole you are by how you drive.

From the highway to a grocery store parking lot, and all the way to a parking space in an apartment complex, the way people use their car speaks volumes about them as a person.

If I were to ask you, when does a wrench become a deadly weapon? You'd probably think, when someone decides to cave another's skull in with the wrench. Easy, right? It's how you decide to use the wrench.

Ok, if we go backwards and I ask, what keeps a butter knife from being an instrument of murder? You're probably thinking, when you use it for its intended purpose, like spreading nasty-ass avocado on your toast.

It's the same thing for your car. When you are following the rules of the road, driving unproblematically, and taking appropriate cautionary measures, your car is a tool doing exactly what it's meant to do. Getting you from point A to B in a safe manner for all involved, including other drivers.

But when you're acting like a taint and treating the road as if you're the most important person on it, you're causing headaches, road rage, and putting other people's lives in danger.

You probably saw highway footage on the news back in April 2025 when a Columbus, Ohio, woman who was 41 years old stopped her car in the middle of I-71 because she missed her exit. Instead of taking accountability for her mistake and going on to the next exit or two, she stopped and waited for a 'clear' avenue to skip over two lanes to get onto the exit she originally wanted but failed to plan for.

In doing so, she caused a three-car chain reaction crash, resulting in minor injuries. Yet her car came out the other end undamaged. How often have you seen people not plan for their exit and shoot across multiple lanes, rather than just owning their mistake and taking the next exit?

We won't even talk about the obviously stupid things like people rolling at excessively dangerous speeds and weaving in and out of traffic, paying no attention to how close people get to the cars in front of them. And I'm not talking about the jackasses who ride people's asses. While every state law varies a little bit, if you ask a lot of people, "How much space should you leave the car in front of you, their answer typically will be something like, "a car length or two."

If you pay attention on the road, it's amazing how many people you'll see sticking to this wildly terrible rule of thumb. Now I'm not going to sit here and preach about how "you should have 3 seconds of space…" when it's simpler than that.

In order to protect yourself, your car, and the person in front of you, don't follow closer than you can stop before seeing what the inside of their asshole looks like.

Easy. Makes sense, right? If there is a car a quarter mile ahead of you moving at 35 mph, why do you feel the need to speed up to them and then continue to move at 35 mph? If you are going to be moving at the same speed you were before, why move? Why close the distance? Why set yourself up with less time to react? If you stayed back, you'd have more than enough time to watch them wipe out before you even needed to slow down.

It's a lack of responsibility for yourself and those in your car.

You're in a parking lot, moving at high speeds, knowing that people are walking about, but you're cutting through the parking spaces because you're too lazy to take the drive lanes around, or you're too impatient to let people walk. You say to yourself, "Cars are moving around, they should be paying attention."

Newsflash, buddy, they won't die if they bump into you. It's a different story when you blast a kid and send them skidding 30 feet. You're the one who is holding everybody else's well-being in your hands when you get behind the wheel.

Maybe you're the twat who's notorious for parking all the way to the right side of a parking spot so that your tubby ass can more comfortably get out of the car while simultaneously making it harder on the poor person who's parked next to you. I bet you'll cry when they ding your shit too.

Then you have the person who so desperately needs to get in front of as many cars as they can because they find themselves so much more important than anyone else, even though, funny enough, we all end up in the same place at the same time.

Your car is the shining light on your ego, and it clearly shows how you think of yourself over others.

When I got my motorcycle, I became obsessed with this YouTuber called DanDan The Fireman. I could probably credit him with being the catalyst who really started moving the cogs in my brain toward accountability.

DanDan takes motorcycle crashes and turns them into a masterclass on personal accountability.

He doesn't waste time blaming cars or bad luck, he calls riders out for the dumb shit they did that set them up to fail.

He'll say, "Yeah, the car pulled out in front of you, but you were flying through a blind spot with zero escape plan. That's on you."

DanDan's whole thing is awareness and ownership, scanning the road, leaving yourself room, preparing for the worst because you respect how fast things can go bad. That's accountability in motion.

It's not about blaming other people; it's about expecting other people to do stupid shit. You can't control the idiot who cuts you off, but you can control how prepared you are for it.

That's the part most people miss: you don't get to control the world, you only get to control your response to it.

Whether it's a bike, a car, or your own damn life, the second you start thinking, "I shouldn't have to" instead of "I could have," you've already given away your power.

The Self Audit

How do you even begin to audit yourself? For me, it started when I was a cable guy. Whenever I finished an install and something wasn't working right, I'd always ask myself something along the lines of "Where did I mess up?"

I'd go through my own mental log from beginning to end, thinking about everything I did and where I could have screwed up or done better. That same thinking has followed me through the years.

Years later, I've increased my pool of questions that I ask myself, and I'll even more readily ask these kinds of questions after nearly every scenario that I want to reflect on:

- "What could I have done better?"

- "Did I ask enough questions?"

- "Was I overconfident, or did I not leave myself room for learning?"

I also have a few that I ask myself in nearly every crossroad at work. When I'm presented with a situation that is 'handled' and doesn't necessarily need further action on my part.

- "Can I confidently say that I'm doing all I can in this situation, or am I taking the easy way out?"

- "Is there more I can do so that I can say that I actually did my best?"

- "Am I or should I be seeing this situation through further than I already am or than the people around me are?"

These last few can truly help separate you in an environment where your actions and throughput have an effect on your customers and coworkers.

You'll know you're asking yourself the right questions when it doesn't feel good. When you start feeling defensive, when you're hitting your own nerve, that's the discomfort zone you want to get comfortable in. That's where you start learning. That's where you'll learn more from yourself or open the door for others to give you feedback that you can use in the future.

When you start becoming more comfortable asking yourself the hard questions, you can begin attacking the hard habits that are keeping you stuck. I call these behaviors, mindsets, and tendencies, The Brutal Truths.

PART 2:
THE BRUTAL
TRUTHS

Nobody is Coming

Here's the first brutal truth: nobody is coming to save you. Your personal responsibility is not transferable, and nobody else can live your life for you. There is no one else who can make your decisions, face your consequences, or tackle your fears and anxieties.

My experience with 75Hard & Live Hard was a perfect example of this, as the rules were laid out in front of me, but I was the only one who could make or break it. Life would throw wrenches in the plan nearly every day, but I was the only one who was going to check off every box. Nobody was coming to do my workouts, read my book, or do my charitable acts. Nobody.

Waiting for someone else to step in removes your ownership and control of the situation. If you want change, you are going to have to be the one to make it.

And here's the worst part: most people in your life probably don't care to see you progress; some will even resent it. That's right. We don't live in a fantasy world where everybody wants everybody else around them to succeed. For those in your life who aren't truly in your corner, your steps forward mean they are falling behind. You'll get shunned or judged for bettering yourself by those who already see themselves as better than you. They aren't on the same path and won't see things the way you will.

Simply put, some people don't want to be saved; they want someone to drown with.

Because of that, understanding that you are in charge of yourself and your feelings is incredibly freeing, yet also lonely, all at the same time. We'll dig further into how self-accountability affects your relationships and perceived friendships in the later part of this book. Spoiler Alert: You're going to lose some friends. And that's okay.

The Rescue Myths

I like to think about the idea of waiting for rescue as two different mindsets: the Big Dream Bullshit (Fantasy Rescues), and the little daily stalls that keep you stuck (Micro Rescues).

Have you ever found yourself not just daydreaming about the lottery but actively hoping for it? "If I win big on one of these scratch-offs, so much will be better." Or maybe the new year has come, and you're anxiously waiting for the tax return because it's going to "fix" something.

These are Fantasy Rescues, big hopes, or wishes that life will fix itself without our own personal action. Sorry, bud, it probably won't happen. Waiting for "the market to turn around" or for inspiration to strike so that you'll finally "get serious" is a formula for procrastination and disappointment.

Band-aid solutions are what these are, and the moment that tax return comes through or that scratch-off hits, your poor decision-making habits are going to put you right back in the spot you are in now, unless you decide that it's time to make the more complex financial moves. That housing market you're worried about? If you had been making smarter moves earlier, you'd be in a better position now to accommodate.

We can't wait for some big thing to happen to improve our lives. We have to do it ourselves, making one decision at a time every day.

You've probably heard the quote, "If you're not part of the solution, you're part of the problem." Mostly repeated in modern politics, but it's often credited back to the 1960s, when Eldridge Cleaver, an American writer, political activist, and one of the early leaders of the Black Panther Party, was active. The quote at the time emphasized that taking no action was seen as enabling injustice.

While it still has its place in politics in 2025, I see it nearly everywhere in our day-to-day lives. So often, we want to complain about the world, other people, or our environment, yet we do nothing to fix it. Why waste the emotional energy to get worked up over something when that energy could be spent on a solution?

How often have you heard something along the following lines? Maybe you've said one or two of these yourself:

- Complaining about the apartment complex's maintenance but not reporting issues.

- Remarking about the condition of local parks or the neighborhood but never volunteering or donating.

- Getting frustrated with your child's organizational skills but not teaching them differently.

- Hoping your partner "figures out" how to improve the relationship instead of initiating the talk.

- Wishing someone else would start a meetup group so you can join it.

- Blaming weight and health on genetics while refusing to change daily habits.

These are what I call Micro Rescues. Small things that you wish someone else would do that would improve your life, preventing you from needing to put in the work.

Why are people so quick to complain, just for the sake of complaining, and yet they aren't willing to take action? Is it laziness? Lack of knowledge or experience? Perspective? The incessant need to whine about fixable things is nauseating.

This same behavior is typically all over the workplace as well. Somewhere that you are being paid to act and think like a grown-ass adult, yet somehow this is where you find the biggest crybabies who constantly need someone else to change their diapers. And even after someone does, they follow up by complaining that it's too tight.

Here's the annoying yet beneficial part, though. You can use their whining and inaction to your advantage. Those people who want to complain about how something is or how it works but don't want to do anything to fix it? They shine a light on doers and people who produce results.

I will never condone climbing a ladder by stepping on others, but once you see and acknowledge that their poor attitudes can make your neutral attitude shine a little brighter, you're ready to take the next step towards productivity and growth. This is when you can go through the workplace as a problem-solver, not a problem-enabler.

We'll talk more later on how the world rewards results, not effort, and how these situations are ripe for the picking to produce results where others just whine and bitch about things. People love to whine in groups, and it's natural to complain about a boss, a schedule, or a process.

See if you've heard anything similar in the workplace:

- Complaining that a work process is inefficient but never offering a solution.

- Griping about the team's poor communication instead of setting an example.

- Wishing your boss would lead better instead of taking the initiative yourself.

- Hating how meetings are run but never suggesting a new structure.

- Complaining about outdated software or action plans, but never researching alternatives.

- Wishing the company would instill more training opportunities instead of pursuing your own development.

- Waiting for someone else to take the lead on a safety issue that everybody knows about.

- Hoping someone else will deal with a consistently difficult customer instead of stepping up and doing it yourself.

Every single one of these examples shares the same common theme. "Someone else needs to fix this." But if no one does, are you still going to sit there and cry?

Own It Now, Not Later

"But Niiiiick, how could I have made smarter moves before to get a house? I'm only 19?"

Obviously, you should have started saving your allowance. Is it really that hard?

But let's be real. There can be certain circumstances that add a level of difficulty to your goals. But that doesn't mean we wait for life to fix them for us. It means we accept the position we are in and take control here and now. Recognizing that we're young and building our wealth, credit, and financial literacy, education needs to start now, not later.

I, for one, did not do any of that. I graduated from high school and immediately fell on my face. I got two credit cards, racked them up, and didn't pay for them. Started college at ITT Tech, didn't finish, then avoided those bills for years. Followed by doing lease-to-own furniture, getting an apartment I could barely afford, and eventually needing to move back in with my grandparents. My poor spending habits put pressure on my family as I had to consistently ask for money to turn my lights back on or to put gas in the tank so that I could get to work.

These habits followed me for years. But I was getting more responsible little by little. However, every day I imagined the better life I would have. "It'll turn around. Somehow." And you know what, it would. Year by year, I would get just a little bit better, a little more mature. But that's all it was, just some maturity as life would teach lessons the way life does, with a kick in the ribs.

Although growth was there, it was small and incremental. At the rate I was going, the version I saw of myself wouldn't be around until I was 80.

Just because you're in a slump in this moment doesn't mean it's a bad time to start pulling things together and changing the way you go about your daily decisions. It's actually the BEST time. There is no better time to look up and climb. You may think you are at rock bottom right now, but trust me, rock bottom has a basement. Stop waiting for some big life event to turn your shit around.

So let me repeat it: nobody is coming. Not to rescue you. Not to motivate you. Not to fix the mess you made. This world will hand you every excuse to stay where you are, and it'll even make it feel comfortable. But that comfort is a trap.

It's a padded failure. The longer you sit in it, the harder it gets to stand.

You keep waiting for a life-changing moment, a sign, a break, a shove in the right direction, but that moment is already happening. Right now. You're just ignoring it because it doesn't come with fireworks and theme music. It comes with a mirror. And it's uncomfortable as hell.

Help Is Okay, But Don't Count on It

Now, while this chapter is all about doing the work yourself and digging out of the grave you are burying yourself in, it doesn't mean you can't accept a hand from time to time. Sometimes it's nice for someone to hand you a shovel.

My old boss-turned-friend, Mike, did that very thing for me. I was staring at a mountain of debt in front of me, with the comfort of avoidance behind me. Mike didn't carry me up that mountain, but he handed me the gear to start climbing it. The harness (the snowball method), the shoes (the basics of a foundation), the rope (accountability and protection), and the map (a simple and clear plan).

The climb was still mine alone. I was the one who still had to take every step. Steps that I'm still making to this day, but with new perspectives and gear that I've picked up along the way.

Now, before you start waiting to act because you're thinking, "Oh man, I need to find that person to help push me over the edge first...."

Right here, this book you're reading. I'm the Spartan kicking you over that edge.

Many people lean on others, emotionally, financially, and even physically. Not because they truly can't act, but because it shields them from accountability. As long as someone else is helping, they can tell themselves, "It's not my fault." However, that crutch quickly becomes a dead weight, preventing real growth.

You are far more capable than you admit; you don't need someone to do it for you.

Choosing to depend on others when you don't need it is a sneaky form of self-sabotage, creating the illusion of safety while dragging down those around you. The longer you let them do it, the more you expect it, and the more your "friends" begin to resent you for it. Soon you'll find yourself being alienated for the wrong reasons.

Understand this: Tools are great. Guidance is useful. But if you're sitting in the dirt, staring at the shovel someone handed you, and crying because they didn't dig for you, that's on you. This whole book is a pile of tools. But I won't dig for you. You've got to grab the handle and get to work.

Climbing Out Alone

Don't mistake this for some self-righteous motivational poster crap. This isn't about pretending life's fair or easy. It's not. You might be carrying trauma. Regret. Debt. Pain. That sucks, and I respect it. But it doesn't change the truth. No one else will do the work for you. They might spot you; they might walk beside you, but they won't carry you. And if they do? You won't grow from it.

You will never become the person you're supposed to be by sitting around hoping life turns itself around. Growth requires discomfort. Progress demands action. And discipline—honest, gritty, unsexy discipline—is how you win this thing. Not talent. Not luck. Not inspiration. Just relentless forward motion.

So, what now?

Now, you stop waiting. You stop fantasizing. You stop hoping that something out there will spark the change. Because it's not out there, it's your next choice. Your next step. Your next refusal to stay soft. You don't need a rescue. You need to rescue yourself, and you are fully capable of doing that, whether you believe it yet or not.

Nobody is coming.

Good.

Now it's your turn to show up.

- φ   Help isn't coming, and it doesn't need to be.
- φ   Radical self-responsibility is the cure for victimhood.
- φ   Every excuse is a surrender of control.

Excuses vs. Truths

Excuses	Truths
I just need someone to push me.	You're too lazy to push yourself.
I don't know where to start.	Anywhere is better than standing still.
Someone will notice my effort eventually.	No one's watching, do it anyway.
It's not fair what I've been dealt.	Life doesn't play fair; it plays for keeps.
I'm waiting for the right time.	There is no right time. There's just now.
It shouldn't be this hard.	That's what makes it worth doing.

Challenge Question

If no one ever helped you again, what would you do next?

You're Not Waiting. You're Hiding.

Procrastination. Some say it's the killer of discipline, but really, it's the symptom of not having any. Procrastination is everywhere in our lives. The consequences of leaving this unchecked can range from not being able to finish your homework and getting a reduced grade to losing your kids to CPS because you didn't make your car payments, it got repo'd, and you used it as an excuse to not be able to work and provide for them.

We all procrastinate a bit. It's basic to prioritize one thing over another based on how much we care about it. However, taking control of your life involves realizing and being aware of when you prioritize a *want* over a *responsibility*.

I'll repeat that again for those who are skimming: Self-accountability and responsibility prioritize what you *need* over what you *want*.

The critical thing to remember, and the whole theme of this book, is recognizing those habits and actions. There are hundreds of ways to combat them, but until you see, hear, or feel those habits in a way that connects, you'll struggle to begin working on a fix.

The 5-Minute Couch Decision

Let's envision a scenario in which procrastination affects us in a way that, on the surface, seems like an annoyance, but not a problem. One that doesn't have immediate consequences.

Think of the last time a cool or fun opportunity came around, but you didn't act on it when you should've. You missed out. We've all had that happen, and it sucks. Sitting at home when you know you could've been out on some grand adventure. Or lunch with the family, sharing laughs and memories.

Maybe a music festival is coming to town, and some coworkers have been talking about it, and you're interested in attending. You're new to the job or city, and you're looking for ways to connect with the new team. Lying on your couch, you're checking the prices of the tickets they were talking about. Prices aren't bad at all. But damn, your wallet is by the front door where you put it and your keys whenever you get home. You don't need to grab them now, you think to yourself.

There are no "Only so many left" warnings like the other sections, so you've got time to grab them the next time you think about it. You know that you should just get up and finish this, but you're comfy, and there's no rush. So, you ignore that voice in the back of your head. You've done it before, and it's worked plenty of times.

But that little voice only exists because it hasn't worked before. That version of you yearning to be better is yelling at you. You just aren't listening… again.

Wednesday comes around, and the tickets slip your mind until later in the day. But you're at a buddy's place playing some board games and don't want to interrupt the fun. You'll just get them on Friday. That works better anyway because it's payday. What you don't know is that the stage-front sections have sold out, and the general admission grass section, farthest from the stage, is selling fast as well.

This is when we should stop to question our laziness and social angst. Would your friends really mind if you paused for half a second to ensure you handled something you care about?

Fast forward to Friday, and you are at your work computer—time to buy those tickets.

Well, shit. The 3-Day Admission tickets are already sold out. Double shit, there's no single Saturday or Sunday tickets left either. The only front-stage tickets left are VIP tickets for Friday, but those are too far out of your budget.

Guess you're stuck with the grass area… gone.

You've missed your opportunity.

"Hey, man!" your buddy comes up behind you. "You going to the festival? That's awesome! Can't wait to see you there!"

Well, that's awkward. There goes your day. You had the five minutes it would have taken to buy the tickets the other day, but chose not to. And why? Because you didn't want to get off the couch? Hell, you had multiple opportunities to get those tickets, but you didn't. Now you're sad and kicking yourself.

Aw, poor baby. Need a hug?

Now you're in the dumps and your performance is suffering. You're embarrassed to tell your friends that you couldn't get tickets. You've got the choice to come clean and feel the shame that your own procrastination caused this heartache, or you could lie. You don't really need to tell them that you were lazy, right?

Listen, if I have to explain to you, a grown adult, why lying your way through this is immature and is the opposite of self-accountability... oh buddy.

Most of us have had some unfortunate consequences like this in our lives. Not a horrible ordeal, but a shitty situation nonetheless. But even though this was simply a missed opportunity, chances are that you're procrastinating on other things. Things that are piling up.

The Domino Effect

The parasite of procrastination nourishes itself like a leech. One delayed task leads to a poorly made decision, which is followed by stress that perpetuates more responsibilities that are put off, and the domino effect just keeps going.

We view these as singular events because we experience them firsthand. But if we zoom out and look at our lives and mindsets from a bird's-eye view and follow the timeline of our feelings and the "I'll do it tomorrow," we can see just how often we hold ourselves back.

You're on your way to your computer to do a little gaming, and you eye those three or four dishes in the sink that could be loaded and get the dishwasher started. But you pass them up, why? You know you're going to grab yourself something to eat later and just add to that pile. Take a few seconds to get it done, and it won't be hanging over your head that you have dirty dishes or a dirty kitchen. If the filth sitting there doesn't bother you at all until it's inconvenient, you're gross, just saying.

In no situation is watching that TV show, playing that game, or scrolling through those videos more important than attending to the responsibilities of your health, finances, relationships, or overall happiness.

Here's another interesting and more harmful example of procrastination.

You're a skilled individual with a talent in your field, but things happen, budgets get cut, and you're laid off. You keep telling yourself it's not the biggest deal. You'll apply to more jobs within the week once the shock wears off. You've got a savings account and the experience to find new work in your field. You just need to fix your résumé first. Consider refining or polishing your cover letter. Hell, maybe even take a new course so you can stand out. Those job postings aren't going anywhere. And if they do, there will be others.

That was two months ago. At first, it felt like a blessing, a break you didn't know you needed. You caught up on sleep. Reorganized the place and got back into some old hobbies. You told yourself you'd enjoy the downtime "just for now." During which, you've held a few part-time jobs that lasted just long enough to say to people you had a job. All this to prepare yourself to hit the ground running.

But either by choice, excuse, or further procrastination, that ground never came. Whoops.

Days blurred into each other. The urgency wore off, replaced with the soft, numbing comfort of routines that didn't challenge you. Wake up late. Scroll. Watch some YouTube. Tell yourself, "Just one more episode." By this point, you aren't even thinking about your LinkedIn. You make a snack, go to that lame-ass, part-time job again for three or four hours, done.

Now, a few months later, your savings are drained and resources strained. The rent is late, and your significant other has started asking questions you didn't want to answer. "How's the job search going?" they'd ask, gently at first. Then more sharply. "You didn't even look today, did you?"

"We can't keep living like this," they repeat.

You told them they didn't understand how hard it was, the pressure, the fear of rejection, the weight of not knowing where to start. But deep down, you knew it wasn't the world that was hard. It was you who avoided it. But that feeling was deeper than you were willing to dig. So, you blamed everything else.

Then the eviction notice came.

Your partner left. You've created stress in your other relationships with friends and family, all of whom are tired of supporting your shit. Depression hit shortly thereafter, if not already present, followed by more excuses. The spiral continues.

That's the thing about procrastination: it doesn't blow your life up in one big, dramatic explosion. It rots everything slowly. Quietly. You don't even notice the smell until it's in your clothes.

Your parents don't want you back in the house, again. Thirty-five years old, once on track for a promotion and moving up in the world, now wondering where you are going to sleep tonight.

That's your false "wake up." You convince someone to borrow their laptop to update your résumé. Finally done, but now there's an employment gap. You're getting passed up for other candidates with more recent experience. Finding a job is now far harder than it would have been.

And you know, all of it could've been avoided if you had just moved—even one inch forward. Suppose you had just said "no" to comfort a few more times; if you had just taken the next step while the world was still closer, within reach.

Procrastination didn't take your life overnight. You took it choice by choice.

The Biological Cop-out

Here's where people love to get cute with science. They'll read some medical research about how avoiding something that causes discomfort can trigger the release of dopamine in your brain and amygdala. Basically, making you feel "good" for avoiding the hard thing. They'll use that to say, "It's not me, it's my brain chemistry."

Yes, researchers at the University of Calgary found that chronic procrastinators show more activity in the amygdala, the brain's fear and emotion center, and weaker links to the prefrontal cortex, the part responsible for mature decision-making. But that doesn't mean you're broken. It means your brain has gotten really good at rewarding you for avoiding hard things. You have literally trained yourself to feel better by doing worse.

So, it is you. The science doesn't excuse you; it proves how long you've been lying to yourself. It's not an illness, it's conditioning. Like any bad habit, it only changes when you stop feeding it. The science isn't your get-out-of-jail card; it's the evidence that you've built the jail yourself.

The Health and Fitness Lie

Gym procrastination. The mecca of "not today, tomorrow." This one requires commitment, discipline, and worst of all... consistency.

Well, hear me out, you overripe banana. We all want a long life where we die from old age. But the stats don't lie. The chance of someone reading this and dying from heart failure is higher than any other cause of death. Is that going to be you? No? Then, at the end of this chapter, get up and go on a fucking walk. Simple.

"I'm going to wait until the new year!"

"I'm going to start on Monday!"

"I'm going to wait until my ankle feels a bit better."

"I'm going to start after vacation."

Sound familiar? Is simply going for a walk for a couple of minutes and moving your body a significant lifestyle change that can't happen today? Why does it have to start on New Year's? Because it's cute and trendy? Get over yourself. If it's worth doing, then it's worth doing now.

"But Niiiiiick, the premiere is on tonight, and all my friends are going to be talking about it tomorrow, and I don't want my friends to be upset that I didn't see it. I'll just work out tomorrow instead."

Okay, I get it. You'll receive no pressure from them if you don't work out, but you will if you miss your show. But what's going to be the excuse tomorrow? Huh? What lie are you going to tell yourself next time that will justify skipping another walk? And your "friends," we'll talk more about this in a later chapter, but if they really cared about you and your commitment to self-betterment, do you think it would really bother them that you held off on the premiere to handle your responsibilities? If so, you may need to do some inner-circle cleanup.

We don't just put off movement. We also put off eating like adults.

We'll say, "I'll start eating clean after the weekend," or "Once the bottle is gone, I'll stop drinking." You're not planning, you're postponing.

We'll scroll through recipes, follow fitness influencers, and bookmark "healthy" food options. Yet never follow through. Or we'll get over the line, go to the grocery store, and still fumble the ball somewhere else down the line, much like I did the other week.

Recently, I spent the better part of a few hours meal-prepping some chicken. However, I had not noticed that my rice had expired. The chicken was done, and I had nothing else to do that day besides veg out, work on this book, and/or finish the meal prep with some rice. I didn't leave the house for the rest of the day. A week later, after forgetting the rice multiple times, I now had chicken in the fridge that was no longer good to eat. That wasn't the intention, but there I was with wasted time, effort, and money.

That's the funny thing about procrastination: it always feels small in the moment. Just a quick delay, but somewhere it always bites you in the ass.

The Long Game of Avoidance

"But Niiiiiiick, I want to do better. I'm just stuck in a rut right now."

...How are you going to get out of that rut without doing anything about it? You're not stuck. You're stalling and avoiding the hard work because it's just that: hard. "Stuck" sounds innocent. Harmless. Like something that just happened to you. But most of the time, you're not stuck. You're choosing not to move. You're overthinking, doubting too long, and planning too perfectly. Progress doesn't stall from lack of ability; it stalls from lack of action. And calling it "stuck" is nothing less than letting yourself off the hook, falsely committing yourself to betterment and then shitting on it.

If your friend or loved one kept putting you off time and time again, how would you feel? Would that make you feel important and worth their time? Would you feel like they actually have your best interests at heart? No! Then why are you treating yourself like that?

Every single delay is a broken promise to yourself, and you're actively sabotaging the person you want to become. You're running away. You tell yourself you're just taking a breather, recharging, resetting, waiting for the "right time." Bullshit. What you're really doing is lying to yourself in a voice that sounds soothing, so you won't feel guilty about standing still.

But you know the difference between rest and avoidance. Real rest comes after effort. This is just an attempt to avoid the responsibility you should've already handled. You're not recharging. You're rotting.

That short nap or that hour of scrolling through videos and newsfeeds, it all adds up. Not to progress, but to pain, regret, and disappointment. Each missed opportunity, poor effort, late payment, rushed project, and last-minute stress takes a chip of confidence out of you and replaces it with doubt and sorrow.

One of the reasons I placed this chapter near the front is that it is at the forefront of an individual's likelihood of success versus failure.

Procrastination isn't passive—it's corrosive. Every day you wait, the tasks grow heavier. Your energy drains. Your guilt builds. What was once a 15-minute chore becomes a mental mountain to climb. Delays turn simple shit into monsters. And every time you wait, you reinforce the belief that the work is bigger than you.

That's how you shrink, not all at once, but choice by choice.

Procrastination doesn't only rob you of productivity and results; it steals your peace of mind. Think about how often you've lain awake at night, mentally replaying what you didn't get done, or waking up with anxiety gnawing at your gut because of yesterday's delays. Those postponed tasks live rent-free in your head, cluttering your thoughts, distracting your focus, and undermining your confidence. Eventually, procrastination doesn't just impact the task you're avoiding; it quietly erodes your mental well-being, leaving you stressed, restless, and emotionally drained.

Don't look up one day and realize your whole life has shrunk because you waited for a feeling that never showed up.

- φ Procrastination isn't just laziness; it's comfort wearing a mask.
- φ Every delay feels harmless in the moment, but small hesitations compound.
- φ The longer you wait to act, the heavier the task becomes.
- φ

Excuses vs. Truths

Excuses	Truths
I work better under pressure.	You don't. You've just trained yourself to panic instead of preparing.
I need to be in the right mindset first.	The right mindset comes from doing, not thinking.
I'll know when the timing's right.	Timing becomes right once you move.
I need to think it through more.	Thinking is the comfort zone of procrastinators.
I've got too much going on.	You always will, that's not new, that's life.

Challenge Question

What's the one thing you've been "meaning to do" that's quietly eating away at you, and what's your excuse for not doing it today?

You Don't Deserve Shit

Over the past couple of years, we have seen an emergence or a redefinition of the word "entitlement." Before COVID, the word was reserved for the rich folk in their large houses and their disconnection from society. You'd pin entitlement to the fancy lady driving her BMW or the kid with his brand new Jeep Wrangler. Thinking things like, "Oh, must be nice having a rich husband," or "I bet mommy and daddy paid for that."

And while that may still hold true for a number of them, the word "entitlement" has found its way to us low-class types. The wave of "I'd like to talk to your manager because I am whoever I think I am" caught the internet by storm. And we hilariously began labeling these people as the infamous *Karens*. (cue screaming)

(Apologies to all Karens out there, but it is what it is. Try a different haircut?)

We've all seen that person in public to some varying degree. The person who acts as if they are owed something, even though both of you are standing at the same counter of a McDonald's at 8 a.m. on a Sunday morning.

"But Niiiiiiick, I drive an eight-year-old car and work a middle-class job. I'm nowhere near entitled. My parents weren't rich, so I had to pay for my own college. I deserve—"

Shut the fuck up, Karen.

Here's a quick list of the things that the real world of success and failure couldn't give a damn about:

- Where you grew up.

- The neighborhood you were raised in.

- Your traumatic childhood.

- Your parents' divorce.

- Your race or ethnicity.

- Your gender or what you identify as.

- Your pronouns.

- Your sexual orientation.

- That your boss is a jerk.

- That you didn't go to college.

- That you did go to college and now have debt.

- That your life has been harder than most.

None of that guarantees success.

None of that earns you a pass.

None of that means you're owed a damn thing.

You're an adult. You need to take off the diaper and accept the fact that you absolutely, without a doubt, do NOT *deserve* a fucking thing in this world. You aren't owed anything by anybody but yourself.

Your situation is not an excuse.

Suffering Isn't Currency

Life isn't going to give you handouts.

People often like to blame their upbringing or childhood as a reason why they are owed an advantage or a helpful push up the hill.

Suffering isn't currency, and struggle does not belong on a scoreboard. You can't go your whole life quoting some traumatic event and believe that to be your ticket to progress.

Many people walk around thinking that because they have struggled, they're somehow owed something. They won't always say it out loud, but the way they carry themselves speaks volumes. Like the world should cut them some slack just because they've seen or been through some shit. Even if it was their poor choices that put them there. That's entitlement, even if it's wrapped in pain. Just as the upper class feels entitled to comfort simply because they were born into wealth, someone who has suffered might feel entitled to relief, opportunity, or a break just because life has been hard.

The world isn't designed to treat you better because you've been through the wringer, and it doesn't need to be. It is your responsibility to take that suffering and either turn it into a strength or decide that it will no longer have any impact on your life. Otherwise, it will continue to eat away at you, and the rest of us will move on. Pain doesn't make you special; it just makes you human. What you do with it defines you.

Ownership vs. Expectation

In my late twenties, I remember talking to my now-wife about different memories from my childhood. I shared memories of visits with my birth dad, recalling how he could be fun at times, but also how he wasn't always so much. My parents split when I was young, so my brother and I would stay with him occasionally before we packed up and moved to New Orleans. It was while describing flashbacks to Rachel about the times we spent with him that I made a connection that had never really crossed my mind before. Now, this is from the memory of a child, mind you, but my dad was an angry guy, sometimes seeming as though happiness was a rarity. But looking back and remembering the punishments he would dish out if we ever acted out of place would send new age "gentle parents" into an absolute mental breakdown.

Looking back now as an adult, it's pretty apparent that most of the corrective measures were over the top, and a lot were skirting dangerously close to being on the darker side of physical abuse.

I was an angry pre-teen and teenager, but I never remember tying anything to that. I remember going to therapy for a little bit, but it was mostly to balance my emotions with my ADHD. Still, nothing ever surfaced about that.

Did that show itself in my angry teen years? I don't know. But as a grown man, there's not a single piece of me that it weighs on, or a decision that it influences.

And why should it? I have my own life, with its own wins and losses, driven by my own decisions. Why should I let that *trauma* dictate how people should treat me or what I'm *owed*? Or, thinking in more recent years, with some bouts of depression and massive amounts of self-doubt, why should the world show me compassion because I was a little sad?

It's not your problem, it's mine.

But I bring all this up because it's important to separate ownership from expectation. Just because something bad happened doesn't mean something good is automatically owed to you in return. Life doesn't settle emotional debts like that.

Effort vs. Results

Yes, sometimes we get lucky; sometimes the stars align, and things do, in fact, fall into our laps unintentionally, and we reap the benefits. However, these are typically temporary and shouldn't be planned for.

There's an interesting saying that goes, "Life doesn't reward effort; it rewards results." The idea is that even if you work harder and longer than the guy or girl next to you day in and day out, it doesn't mean a thing if that other person is continually outperforming you in whatever metric or standard you're being held to.

We see this so often in the working world, where people believe they are owed more because of how "hard" they work or how much "effort" they put in. They think they deserve that pay bump, promotion, respect, or opportunity simply because they *tried really, really hard.* Backed by their point of view, where they see the other individual only put in half or a quarter of the effort.

Buckle up, Buttercup. Here's a basic example of where your point of view blinds you into thinking that because you worked harder, you should automatically reap the benefits.

You and Sam are given a side task of equal difficulty, time commitment, and deadline. You hit some roadblocks because there were things you didn't know how to do or hadn't mastered. However, you learned and completed the project on time, despite spending many hours both on and off the clock.

Sam, you noticed, was slacking around with their side project. They were handling their day-to-day only with some other side stuff, but weren't putting in nearly as much focus on the task that the two of you were assigned. Unexpectedly, your boss moved up your deadlines. Yet somehow Sam still produced impeccable results. Their project made yours look like a middle school science fair project.

Your boss thanks and recognizes both of you for your hard work. Unfortunately, you hear that Sam was given a ton of extra kudos from some of the other key stakeholders. People who you would love to know that you exist. How did this happen? You clearly worked harder. You put in far more effort. And you probably spent as many hours working on it. Their end result was a little bit better, but they didn't put nearly as much effort into it as you did.

This is the part we all struggle with. Taking a step back and looking at the whole picture. Really trying to see it from someone else's point of view. Your coworker didn't put in nearly as much effort as you did, and that's simply because your 100% was just as effective and produced the same results as their 70%.

Remember how you had to learn and build new skills. Sam has already developed those. Those new networking relationships and work partnerships you needed to make? Sam had those people in their back pocket already. The exact project you were working on, Sam had done something similar two years ago, and still had the resources handy. They were able to quickly and efficiently use their experiences and tools to accomplish their goals in a manner that exceeded expectations.

So while you were responsibly doing your work and putting in the time, Sam was, too. Remember how Sam was also handling the day-to-day tasks and other projects? To your boss, that shows that Sam has the necessary capacity to handle more responsibilities.

You did nothing wrong; you did a great job with the tools and skills you had at the beginning, but in this scenario, you don't *deserve* more than your counterpart. But guess what, you're more of an asset now than you were before. Next time, you'll be able to accomplish things more efficiently and effectively, with less effort. Next time, you just may be in Sam's shoes. Maybe two years ago, Sam was in your shoes.

Now, that doesn't mean you're next up, though. If you're the ambitious type, what happens when a new guy comes in and he is an absolute killer on Excel, and you just learned how to merge rows? If Excel is a program you use frequently at work, consider dedicating some focus to it and setting yourself up for success. Additionally, just because you've been at the company longer doesn't automatically mean you deserve the accolades over the new guy. Yes, time-in-seat does have weight, but it shouldn't be a replacement for reliability and effectiveness. It is your duty to earn your rewards, not expect them to be given to you.

I fondly remember spending a lot of my childhood in Little League sports. One year in particular, I had signed up for my first and only attempt at baseball. I was around 10 or 12 years old. Long story short, I wasn't very good at all. Left fielder. What I also remember is that our team was absolute garbage. We were the "Franco's," named after a local mega health club that was sponsoring us. If memory serves, the only game we won was the very last one; every other one was a blowout.

At the end of the season, we had a pool party with pizza and ice cream at the health club, like teams do. But what always sticks in my mind was the trophies we had gotten. Now, by this point, I had already had my fair number of trophies and ribbons from other Little League teams, but this was the first one that I ever looked at and thought to myself, "The fuck? Why?"

Yes, even in my youth, I had a mouth that wasn't for the faint of heart. *Thanks, Mom.*

It was the most embarrassing trophy I had ever gotten. While I was too young to know that it was called a participation trophy, I was old enough to realize that I hadn't earned this. I wasn't even a teenager yet, and I was already able to make the connection that my lack of effort, and our team's lack of results, did not warrant this piece of bronze-painted plastic. *Oh, goody, we won ONE game!* Get outta here.

In researching this book, I found a really cool study led by Professor Corey Cusimano and his team from the Yale School of Management. This study challenges the idea that most people value their own effort over their results.

Supported by his two Ph.D. students, Jin Kim and Jared Wong, the team set out to gauge how people pay themselves based on effort versus results. They tested a large number of participants across Italy, Great Britain, the United States, and France. The individuals were assigned easy or complex tasks using Prolific, an online research tool. Afterwards, they were given a range of pay in which they would have to be given to participate in the study another time. Interestingly enough, those who produced better results, whether the tasks were difficult or easy, chose a higher pay amount than their counterparts who produced lesser results.

It turns out that even when people sweat and get to choose their own reward, they still know deep down that results matter more than effort.

False Intentions

And that brings us to another uncomfortable truth: Your intentions don't mean shit, either.

Just like effort, meaning well doesn't earn you anything. You don't get credit for what you were *planning* to do or *what you were thinking* about doing. The world doesn't give out participation trophies like my baseball team did.

It's weird that people love to hang their identities on what they *meant* to do. And frankly, it actually loses you respect.

"I meant to apologize."

"I was going to help you."

"I intended to grab you a gift for your birthday."

Cool. But you didn't. You're either lying to me and never actually intended these things, or worse, you gave it a thought, but I wasn't worth your time.

You don't get to demand judgment, patience, or respect from someone because of an action you intended but never accomplished. Get over yourself.

It's even weirder when people act as if they deserve respect or acknowledgment because they DIDN'T do something. You've heard those people, the ones who admit that they had the intention of acting immaturely or disrespectfully but "chose the high road" instead. And because they did, they have that smirk or expectation of respect.

"I was going to leave my cart, but I thought about how that would look, so I put it away." *Ok, why was that even in question to begin with? Lazy ass.*

"I had every intention of taking it easy today at work, but we are kind of busy, so I'll help get through what needs to be done." *Thank you so very much for doing the exact minimal thing we are paying you to do. Work.*

The moment you start thinking you deserve something just because you didn't screw it up, you've already lost the plot. The world isn't grading you on what you could've done wrong; it's watching what you actually deliver. And if all you're offering is the absence of failure, don't be shocked when no one's impressed.

Reality Check

So let's make this simple.

You're not owed anything because you suffered. Not because you worked hard. And not because you meant well. That's not how the world works.

You don't get rewarded for pain; you get rewarded for progress. You don't get ahead because you tried; you get ahead because you delivered. You don't earn respect for *almost*, you earn it for *action*. Every time.

The second you start thinking you deserve something just because life's been hard, or because you put in the hours, or because you tried really, really hard, you've already lost. That's the trap. That's the mindset that keeps people stuck.

Entitlement doesn't move you forward; it keeps you parked in place, waiting for recognition that's never coming.

This world doesn't pay for effort. It pays for results. It doesn't care about your backstory. It cares about what you've done lately. You don't deserve shit.

But you can earn it.

φ Entitlement isn't just a rich-person problem. It's any belief that struggle, status, effort, or intention earns you something over anyone else.

φ The world doesn't owe you a damn thing. It only pays out those who deliver.

φ Hard work without outcome isn't noble, it's inefficient.

Excuses vs. Truths

Excuses	Truths
I've had it harder than most.	So what? That's your fuel, not your free pass.
At least I meant well.	Intent without action is still nothing.
I've earned a break.	You've earned consistency, not comfort.
They should appreciate what I've done.	You're not owed applause for doing the minimum.
I'm due for something good.	Life doesn't owe you balance; it owes nothing.

Challenge Question

What's one area of your life where you're quietly waiting to be rewarded for trying instead of delivering, and what would change if you judged yourself by results instead of effort?

Stop Negotiating with Yourself

You know that little voice in your head? The one that says having pizza tonight is fine, or skipping the workout won't hurt? Maybe you made it to the gym and it's leg day, but that voice tells you that your chest feels fine, so that we can do upper body again. Or it's payday and you've pulled some overtime. You know that you should put some extra payments into debts, but that overtime was hard, so you can treat yourself a little bit first.

Yeah, that voice is your biggest enemy, and its sole purpose is to keep you in a comfort zone of lies. And the worst part, that voice is you! It fuels your procrastination and excuses, but it does it so smoothly that you don't even realize how often it sways your life.

In the 75Hard community, your inner voice is widely coined and referred to as your *"bitch voice."* It's that part of you that negotiates, excuses, and invents reasons to avoid the hard things. I LOVE this term. The rawness and accuracy are unmatched by any other word I can think of. However, I am not interested in getting sued, so from now on, we'll continue to refer to it as our inner voice.

We all know the cartoon version of this. On one of your shoulders is a mini version of you that reflects what you want to be. Dressed in a toga and halo, pointing you toward the more challenging, better path. But on the other shoulder is the version of you that you don't want to be, but their actions are easier and get you what you want. Devil horns, leather jacket, smoking a cigarette while listening to Megadeth, whispering sweet nothings into your ear. *That last part might be just me, though.*

Unfortunately, this is real life, and for some reason, we don't get the angel version of ourselves in our heads, just the other guy. We don't get to see an example of our greater self to help guide us to make the right decisions. We have to envision that and create it ourselves. All the while, our inner voice is sabotaging us at every opportunity.

This voice is the sneakiest and most manipulative part of yourself, and it knows the EXACT things to say to convince you to take the easier routes.

When You're at War with Yourself

I can be a pretty competitive person who thrives on "Doubt me? Watch this" scenarios. During my first run through LiveHard, my inner voice wasn't too loud and was somewhat muted by the need to prove a point. Throw in some momentum and pride, and we ended up with a good win.

However, the second round of 75Hard was brutal. My inner voice grabbed a megaphone and shouted, "Now listen up!"

"You can't do this."

"You're hurting too much. You'll get injured."

"Have the extra calories. No one will know."

"No one will know if you skip."

"You know you won't finish anyway."

The original dialogues were gone. I had already been through this. I knew the commitment, I knew what to expect, and I knew when and where my upper limits were. I'll forever remember that my second round was the most mentally draining run because I was directly fighting myself every day.

"You've done this already."

"You've got nothing to prove."

"You're a fraud."

"Everyone is sick of you and your fake discipline. They think you're arrogant."

Physically, I had the typical aches and pains. Still, mentally I was fighting an internal battle to quit or try again another time every day.

It was on day 28 that I started having serious thoughts about quitting, but I didn't make the decision that day. I would only allow myself to do it if day 35 came around and I was just as miserable. I knew deep down I wouldn't quit. Day 35 would be past the halfway point, and I would be too stubborn to quit by that point. If asked, my wife would say that I'm a glutton for punishment.

So, of course, day 35 came. I had a great run that morning, my weight plateau broke, I got all my water in early, and our team won our hockey game that night. I felt fast on the ice, my ankles felt strong, and I even buried one in the back of the net. How can you quit on a day like that?

I finished that round strong with multiple personal wins over the course of those hard weeks. I never looked back on that day, even though I almost wavered with myself to give in and listen to that inner voice.

Your Word Is Law

Your word to yourself should be law. Would you trust someone else who consistently lets you down or doesn't follow through with their promises to you? No! So why would you do that to yourself? Don't chip away at your own credibility.

It can be easy to do, though, and typically when I hear this, it's because they set themselves up with things they "want" to do, not "have" to do. If you are setting up your self-improvement checklist as a "maybe" checklist, you've already failed from the start.

Deciding to better yourself requires a commitment without negotiation. You know you have the time to get up at 5:00 a.m. instead of 6:00 a.m. And if you do so, you'll be able to better prep for the day.

If you tell yourself, "I'll see what I feel like when that alarm goes off," you have not committed at all, and you're lying. Don't give yourself options; give yourself rules.

A personal rule of mine is that I will never hit the snooze button more than twice. I back this nonnegotiable up with lessons learned from past mistakes because I know that if I do, I will typically push it until I am forced to roll straight from bed and into the car. Tired and disheveled, I won't put much thought into my cleanliness and appearance, which will negatively affect further things simply because I didn't want to open my eyes.

And if that's not enough reason, I also avoid multiple alarms because I don't want to wake my wife and risk her bullying me later.

One unforeseen positive of this nonnegotiable is that even on my off days, my internal clock has learned to get up pretty quickly. Even on my off-days, I'm naturally rolling out of bed around 6 or 7 a.m.

When you give yourself these nonnegotiables, you begin to understand your personal limits and tendencies. You start to recognize when you are truly serious and committed to an idea. This enlightenment can open doors and your mind to new possibilities that before seemed like a far reach.

Every time you give in, you teach yourself that your wants, needs, and goals are flexible and "can wait." How confident are you going to be in your ability to follow through if you keep reinforcing that habit?

But every time you stay strict with yourself, especially when it gets hard or boring, you are instilling a discipline that no drill instructor in the world can give you. Your goals are a priority, and there is no room for compromise.

Call Your Own Bluff

This is how to quiet your inner voice and tell it to go fuck itself.

I want you to challenge your inner voice right now. Go for a walk. Right now. 2 minutes, 5 minutes, 60 minutes. I couldn't care less.

You are reading this book because you want a spotlight on your bad habits. Right now, your inner voice is probably telling you, "I'm not doing that." Or, "I'll do it when I'm done reading."

No, I want you to get up right now and stop reading this book. Get up and go take a walk. A real, dedicated, get-your-legs-moving-a-bit walk. I'll wait.

Now, as I see it, this has gone one of four ways, listed from most to least likely.

a.   You didn't move. *You're rationalizing.*

b.   You went. *You badass.*

c.   You stopped reading for a while and have returned. *Welcome, let's get back on track.*

d.   You quit. *Since you probably aren't seeing this,* 👆.

Nobody is better at negotiating and manipulating your goals than you are. That is why you need to keep a guard up against yourself that is unmovable.

"But Niiiiiiiick, I couldn't get to the gym this morning, and I don't like going in the evening hours. But since tomorrow is typically a rest day, I'll go then."

No, tomorrow is your rest day, the day designed for your rest. Do you think you'd be willing to toss that day away if you were committed and taking your physical fitness as seriously as you tell yourself you do? No, you wouldn't. You would not negotiate away a day in place to let your body heal just because the gym is going to be *a little busy.* You should've gone this morning if that was a problem.

"But Niiiiiiiick, I was going to, but I just need to psych myself up for those early workouts."

No, you don't. You weren't psyching up, you were stalling. You were giving that inner voice just enough wiggle room and time to tell you, "It's too late, we can try again tomorrow."

"We aren't in the right mindset."

"We haven't hydrated enough."

See the pattern yet? You gave yourself the flexibility in your goals, and it took almost no effort to talk yourself out of them.

Here's the favorite one, and I will admit to falling prey to this multiple times.

"But Niiiiiiiiiiick, I'm going to start eating healthy, but I'm going to start after the weekend, or after this event, or after one more pizza."

No, what you're doing is searching for the perfect mood to help make a hard decision feel easy. That "prep" or "right time" is your inner voice fighting you and delaying you from doing a hard thing. It's saying, "Hey, I get it, you're motivated, so am I, we got this! Just not today. Today's not good for me… I mean you. How about this, what if…."

These compromises water down and define your identity, becoming who you are and drowning out who you want to be. We've mentioned a few times how, internally, you lose trust in yourself because you can no longer convince yourself that you'll follow through on your commitments.

Your Word in the Real World

But you're not the only one seeing through the bullshit. Those internal conflicts and negotiations bleed out into the world and your relationships as well.

Even if you follow through with the promises you make to others, they can see when you aren't following through with your personal commitments to yourself. It still hurts your credibility and their trust in you because, in their eyes, how can they trust you with their needs if you can't be trusted with your own?

To them, this negotiation may not sound like weakness; it'll sound logical all the way up until the point you never actually do anything about it.

"I'm sore, and soreness means recovery."

"I should listen to my body."

"I've been working a lot. I should take it easy before I burn out."

As I write this final section, I notice a hint of hypocrisy in it. I am currently on my first real break from work in over a year. A year filled with over 200 hours of logged overtime, plenty of unlogged, and strings of days where my effort and results were over 100% of what is expected of me. Not that I am complaining about any of it—I chose that grind.

However, the week leading up to this vacation, I had mentioned to multiple people that I would be turning off all things work-related and disconnecting. Something I don't do often. I told myself that I was going to give myself the chance to rest, as a burnout was on the horizon.

I have responded to two emails during my vacation so far, read a few others, signed up for overtime, and had multiple conversations with teammates regarding day-to-day work subjects.

Here's where that inner voice tries negotiating with me as I'm writing to you. "But Niiiiiiiiick, you were just reacting to things coming to you."

And?

"You aren't actively checking on things every day."

I took the time to build a new project page on the first day of my vacation.

"But you haven't thought of it since."

(This is me currently turning off all notifications on work-related apps.)

I told myself I would do something, and I didn't. My reset from work and downtime has been half-assed. Is this really going to negatively affect my burnout risk, or how relaxing my vacation has been? No, not at all.

But I have clearly lied to myself. Looking back right now, if I had *promised* myself that I wouldn't do anything work-related, that fucking inner voice would probably say, "Ha, yeah, right."

That's the part that really gets under my skin. The inconsistency in my own word. I can be rock-solid in one area and a complete flake in another. That inner voice knows precisely where to apply pressure. It doesn't waste time arguing with me on things I take seriously.

Those "gray areas" or "it doesn't really matter" promises. Those are precisely the spots that define whether you are disciplined or just a person defined by convenience.

These things might not seem like a big deal in the grand scheme of things, but broken promises, even small ones, accumulate. They reinforce a version of you that bends, that wiggles, that renegotiates when something feels optional. We don't want to be that version. That person doesn't hit goals. That person doesn't follow through.

That's where your inner voice thrives, when your commitment shakes. If you keep your promises loose, you'll keep finding wiggle room. But the more clearly you draw the line, the more power you take back. You want that voice to shut the fuck up? Stack your wins. Prove it wrong. Starve it of opportunities. Beat it into submission with action.

You won't win every time. I sure as hell don't. But this is a war of attrition. And the more battles you win, the more momentum you build.

Don't overthink it.

Don't debate it.

Decide once, then do it.

- ɸ Your inner voice's goal is to protect comfort.
- ɸ Every time you debate a commitment, you train yourself to lose future battles.
- ɸ Discipline is not the absence of weakness; it's being willing to succumb to it.

Excuses vs. Truths

Excuses	Truths
I'll start Monday.	You're not waiting for the right time, you're waiting for it to feel easy.
I'll see how I feel.	If action depends on your feelings, you'll never reach your goals.
I'm just tired.	You're not tired, you're undisciplined.
I've already done enough today.	"Enough" is the anthem of mediocrity.
I'll start fresh next week.	That's code for never.

Challenge Question

Where in your life are you still negotiating with yourself, talking instead of acting?

No One Cares How You Feel

The world doesn't give a fuck about your feelings. Stop waiting for it to care, and start moving like it never will.

Here's the thing that I think most people know but don't admit: the world runs on consequences, not compassion. The clock doesn't slow down because you're overwhelmed. Your landlord doesn't pause rent because you're anxious. The weather, your boss, and your competitors are all operating on input and output. That's not cruelty, that's physics. Life pays out to execution, not emotion.

But instead of accepting that, we built a culture obsessed with emotional validation. We act like feelings are currency. We hand out sympathy where results should live.

Have you ever noticed how often we validate emotions over outcomes just to avoid confrontation? We coddle stress, cradle discomfort, and tiptoe around fragility, instead of doing the obvious, calling someone out when they're just being sensitive.

"I didn't clean the house today. I wasn't in the right headspace."

"I skipped work because my vibe was off."

And somehow, instead of telling people, "I get it, life's hard, just get it done," we are handing out gold stars for emotional weather reports.

Here's a favorite one of mine I experienced firsthand.

A group of friends and I were hanging out one afternoon when we decided we wanted to order some pizza, so we volunteered two of the girls in the group to order it. Unfortunately, the pizza place's website wasn't working, so they had to call in the order. Now, most of us millennials and older probably remember that calling for food delivery was the norm. But for these two, you could've sworn that they were making a cutthroat international business deal by how stressed they got.

However, I had grown accustomed to this behavior from them by this point and didn't think much of it. It was after the phone call, which was only a couple of minutes by the way, that they were so worked up over the ordeal that they had to leave and go to the other room to have a "lie-down" to destress.

Every single one of my flabbers were aghast. The fact that a simple phone call to order some pizza was enough to cause not one, but two young adults to have physical distress makes me worried for our younger generations. And to think, these two were at the time actively involved in vital roles within our community's youth education system.

During this event, my current career role required me to manage multiple facets of aircraft performance, safety, and airspace coordination. I wished that my biggest stressor of the day was talking to another human being to order food.

But stress and anxiety have been weaponized so much that not a single one of us questioned it out loud, even if we were all thinking it. We just let them go to the other room to have a quiet moment after their "traumatic" event instead of "triggering" them into acting like we weren't validating their feelings.

Feelings as Permission Slips

Everyone feels some negative emotions: stress, anxiety, discomfort, depression. It's the way of life, and it's your entry ticket to being human. Even your toughest people on the planet feel things. They just don't let "how I feel" turn into a permission slip for failure.

I'll admit that I have low times, just like anyone else. Call it "seasonal depression" if you want, but I'm no stranger to the 6 a.m. cold and dark drives where I sit there silently behind the wheel, wondering, "What's the point?" Wondering why I'm doing anything at all.

But guess whose problem it is? Mine. No one else's. As grim as some of those mornings feel, I don't reserve the right to expect others to give me a free pass because *I'm a little sad.*

Increasingly, people turn emotions into justification and label them as empowerment.

Here's what it sounds like in real life, because it's never said out loud this bluntly, but it's always there.

"It's ok that I've kind of stunted myself at work because I'm afraid of public speaking. It makes me uncomfortable, and the company shouldn't expect that of me. You know what, the fact that I even tried should earn me some kudos, and because it's not in my job description, I shouldn't even need to be better at it."

That's not emotional honesty, it's more avoidance. What you're seeing isn't vulnerability, it's a performance, a person protecting their comfort and calling it growth.

They aren't blocked by fear; they're hiding behind it.

And it's not just them. We do this everywhere.

"I didn't go to the gym because I wasn't motivated."

"I yelled at my kids because I was stressed."

"I skipped class because I was anxious."

The truth is that your feelings may explain your behavior, but they don't excuse it. Nobody cares if you were tired when you blew the deadline and put everyone else in a tight spot. The outcome is that the work was not completed.

That's what "permission slip" behavior really is: treating your emotions as a hall pass. You hand it to yourself and expect the world to honor it.

That's the mistake. Using your emotions as a weapon to get sympathy instead of results. Confusing the right to feel with the right to demand that everyone else respect the fallout from those feelings.

The Age of Emotional Entitlement

In *The Coddling of the American Mind,* authors Jonathan Haidt and Greg Lukianoff make it painfully clear: we've trained an entire generation to believe that emotional discomfort is equivalent to actual harm. That being challenged is dangerous. That being offended is violence.

That mindset didn't stay confined to college campuses; it bled into workplaces, social circles, and everyday interactions.

And now? We've got grown-ass adults who expect everyone else around them to tiptoe around their feelings so they don't get offended, canceled, or called a bigot. Every disagreement is suddenly "unsafe." Give feedback once, and someone reacts as if you just pulled a weapon.

That's not mental health awareness, that's emotional entitlement.

"I don't feel safe here."

You're in a Starbucks, Tiffany. Not a war zone.

"I'm feeling overstimulated. I don't like it here."

It's called the grocery store. You're not in NYC during rush hour.

"Your tone is aggressive, and I need you to protect my energy."

No, you just have thin skin.

We've softened words like "harm" and "trauma" to the point that *any* emotional discomfort is treated like a human rights violation. We continue validating the meltdown instead of correcting the behavior.

But, as we've been saying, nobody actually cares about your feelings. If you are someone who uses your emotions as a weapon, just know that the world resents you. If your emotional state is so fragile that someone else's *word choice* is so detrimental to your stress level, you truly need to start getting that in check. It only "feels" like everyone cares because you've trained your social media habit and algorithms to put that material in front of you because it grabs your attention.

You don't get to cry "unsafe" because someone at a theme park misgenders you while trying to be polite. Not every social misstep is violence.

Your personal discomfort isn't oppression. Most people don't care who you love, what you call yourself, or what color your skin is; they just want you to stop forcing it into every conversation.

It makes zero sense to put so much emphasis on your feelings when they are so easily bruised. Emotional fragility isn't a badge of honor, and forcing everyone to tiptoe around your labels isn't respect; it's fear. If a label constantly needs policing, it's not stable, and it's forcing people to speak out of fear of retribution instead of genuine respect.

Unfortunately, with every new label becoming some kind of shield, we are seeing every tiny preference become a disorder of some kind, and we have to pretend like it's revolutionary.

If you weren't annoyed or triggered yet, let me toss you a grenade.

Fragility and False Identities

The world doesn't give two shits about your internet-driven self-diagnosis. But before you start typing your defense thread, let's draw a line.

I'm not talking about people with real diagnoses who are actively seeking treatment and trying to live normal, productive lives. Those people are doing the work. Respect to them.

I'm talking about the wave of self-appointed "neurodivergent warriors" who watched a 60-second TikTok and decided they're part of a marginalized medical class because they don't like Velcro or loud noises. Then they turn that into their entire personality and excuse for being unreliable, annoying, or straight-up lazy.

"I don't like it when people chew gum. That's my trauma response."

"My ADHD doesn't allow me to wear shirts with tags."

"I can't eat off colored plates, I'm neurodivergent."

Own Your Sh*t: You're the Problem

Fuck off. Not everything needs a diagnosis. Some things are just quirks, and guess what, you're weird, just like the rest of us. We've reached a point where people want to be broken because broken gets attention. Being functional isn't fashionable anymore; it doesn't earn engagement. Victimhood has become currency, and the exchange rate just keeps dropping.

When every minor inconvenience becomes a "condition," responsibility evaporates. You stop being expected to adapt. You stop being expected to grow. Why would you work on patience or focus when you can just claim a disorder and be done with it? The second you brand your quirks as disabilities, you trade ownership for identity, and that trade always costs you progress.

This isn't about mocking mental health; it's about calling out the people weaponizing it for sympathy and status. When everything becomes a disorder, nothing carries weight. You don't need a label for every inconvenience. You need coping skills.

That's why everyone's walking on eggshells. Nobody wants to offend the next self-appointed advocate with a fragile identity. So instead of honest feedback or objective standards, we give participation trophies and quiet tolerance. And the people who actually need help? They get buried under the noise.

And just when you think the self-victimization couldn't scale any higher, it does. We zoom out and slap a political label on it.

Suddenly, your quirks aren't just personality traits; they're a form of oppression. Your discomfort isn't just a bad day; it's a systemic issue. And you're not just an overly sensitive individual anymore; now you're a martyr for your side of the political aisle.

That's the next evolution of the excuse machine: turning emotional fragility into political identity. And it's just as lazy. And because victimhood sells, it didn't stay personal. It went mainstream. Outrage became marketing. Every cause, every campaign, every platform learned that feelings get more clicks than facts. Suddenly, politics wasn't about progress anymore; it was about who could cry the loudest.

We've created a generation of people who think outrage is a form of activism. You vote once every four years and act like that gives you moral authority to whine about the economy, the job market, or your "lack of opportunity." But here's the truth: your political team isn't going to save you, and the other team isn't what's ruining your life—you are.

This isn't a political book, but owning your shit absolutely extends into how you navigate politics. Responsibility doesn't clock out when you hit the voting booth.

If you base your vote on party loyalty instead of actual issues, you're not informed, you're indoctrinated. Voting blue because it's blue, or red because it's red, doesn't make you righteous. It just makes you loud.

Owning your shit means owning your decisions, especially the ones that come with real consequences. If you scream about how much the system matters but can't name a single candidate outside the two you were spoon-fed, you don't care about the system; you care about belonging.

Tendencies are fine. Loyalty is fine. But when loyalty overrides your ability to think independently, you're not a voter—you're a cheerleader.

And after all the feelings, the labels, the excuses, and the political finger-pointing, one thing never changes: you still have to get up and do the work.

Execution Still Wins

Not everyone is out here screaming about being triggered or needing a safe space. Some have just mastered the art of quiet avoidance. "I'm tired." "I don't think I should have to." "That's not in my job description." They're not throwing tantrums, they're just folding under the weight of mild discomfort. But here's the deal: life doesn't filter responsibility based on your mood or what's technically assigned to you. Growth lives in the stretch zone. If you're consistently mentally clocking out the second something feels inconvenient, you're not protecting your peace; you're stunting your progress. Being tired doesn't exempt you from the grind. Being outside your role doesn't make it someone else's job to care more than you. This is the kind of emotional fragility that wears a button-up and keeps receipts, remaining professional, polite, yet a dead weight to any real progress.

The world doesn't care who you voted for, what you call yourself, or how emotionally valid your TikTok comment section thinks you are. Life responds to execution.

You want to know what's actually inspiring? Not someone flaunting their trauma. Not someone demanding attention for their discomfort.

It's the mom who wakes up at 5 a.m. to work two jobs after chemo.

It's the guy with crippling anxiety who still speaks up in meetings because he knows his family's future depends on it.

It's the athlete who drags their ass into practice every day while their personal life is falling apart and still doesn't use it as a crutch.

That's what owning your shit looks like.

It's not clean. It's not perfect. But it's honest. It's accountable. And it doesn't demand praise for doing what needs to be done.

You can't out-hashtag lack of effort. You can't out-label laziness. You can't out-emotion your own action.

You either show up, or you don't.

You either finish the job, or you don't.

You either own your shit, or you keep trying to sell it to the rest of us like it's someone else's fault.

The world doesn't care how tired you are or how misunderstood you feel. It doesn't even care how much "potential" you have. It cares whether you deliver.

Remember Chapter 1? Nobody's coming. Still true.

It's not your coworker's job to tiptoe around your triggers.

It's not your boss's job to motivate you daily.

It's not the government's job to hand-deliver opportunity.

It's on you. All of it. Always has been. And when you finally accept that, the bullshit starts falling off fast.

In this chapter, we examined how your emotions are perceived and reacted to by the outside world. But in the next chapter, we'll look inward, at how those same emotions affect your everyday decision-making.

- φ The world doesn't respond to your emotions, it responds to your execution.
- φ Feelings can explain behavior, but never excuse it.
- φ Emotional fragility has become a badge of honor, and it's keeping people weak.

Excuses vs. Truths

Excuses	Truths
That's not my job.	Growth starts where your job description ends.
People should respect my feelings.	Respect is earned through behavior, not demanded through emotion.
They should care more.	You're responsible for outcomes, not sympathy.
I don't feel supported.	That's your cue to build self-support.
It's not fair they don't understand.	They don't need to, they're not living your life.

Challenge Question

What's one area of your life where you've been letting your emotions dictate your effort?

Your Feelings Don't Get a Vote

How you've handled a single marshmallow as a kid says a lot about who you've become.

Imagine this: You're five. One marshmallow sits on the table. The adult says, 'You can eat it now, or wait 15 minutes and get two.' One choice. One test.

If you waited, you didn't just earn a second marshmallow. Years later, kids like you scored higher on tests, earned more money, stayed healthier, and handled stress better.

The ones who couldn't wait? Their lives tended to be tougher.

What's the difference? It was just one marshmallow.

They let their feelings vote.

They felt the urge, the impulse, the craving. They acted without logic and on emotion.

You think it's just sweets. However, that impulse doesn't vanish; it evolves into cheap dopamine, credit cards, and diets.

That same impulse shows up when you scroll social media instead of sleeping, spend money you don't have, or pick a fight just to feel heard. It's not about marshmallows anymore; it's about control.

This isn't about ignoring your feelings; it's about refusing to let them run your life.

Not denying your feelings. Not pretending that you don't have them. But learning to move through your life without your emotions or feelings getting a seat at the decision table.

That test revealed what most adults still haven't learned: instant satisfaction and emotional control can't coexist. The same instinct that makes a kid grab the marshmallow early is what makes adults skip workouts, sabotage diets, or fire off texts they regret. We don't outgrow the impulse; we just justify it better.

This chapter isn't about the marshmallow, it's about the muscle, the one that separates how you feel from what you do. Some people never build it, and they pay for it every day in bad decisions disguised as "following their heart."

That's where this next part comes in. Because control isn't something you're born with, it's something you train.

The Three-Reaction Framework

The Marshmallow Test has been around since the 1960s, with newer studies still supporting its findings. The better you are at waiting, the better you handle life.

You've met the people who live on emotion: the ones who crawl back to the toxic ex, skip applying for the job they want, or 'treat themselves' because the day was hard. We all do it sometimes, let feelings steer instead of logic.

Emotions are valid, and it's important to recognize them in our everyday lives and relationships. However, it's just as important to recognize the difference between having a feeling and acting on it.

There's a saying I heard years ago that stuck with me.

"Your first reaction is often what you are conditioned to feel. Your second is what you actually feel. Your third is who you decide to be."

I typically explain it like this:

Your first emotional reaction is often driven by ego, stress, or conditioning. It's the version of you that slams the steering wheel in traffic, fires off a text you shouldn't, or argues online with someone you'll never meet. You snap, roll your eyes, fire back, or shut down, not because it's completely who you are, but because it's what you've taught yourself to do when you feel cornered. It's the survival mode part of you trying to protect your image or pride. It's loud, messy, and fast.

Your second emotional reaction is the pause. That's the deep breath before you say something you'll regret. That small gap between impulse and logic. It's when your brain catches up to your body and says, 'Hold on a second, what's really going on here?' That's when the emotional fog begins to clear a bit. You start thinking instead of just reacting. It's uncomfortable, but it's where honesty lives.

Then comes the third reaction, choice. This is who you decide to be once the smoke clears. It's the version of you that acts with intention instead of instinct. Sometimes that takes five minutes; sometimes it takes a day. But it's always available. The problem is, most people never get there. They stop at the first or second, so they keep living the same emotional patterns on repeat.

The goal isn't to pretend that the first reaction doesn't exist; it always will. The goal is to shrink the time it takes to reach the third one. To train yourself to pause, to question, and to choose instead of react.

It's that simple pause that's saved me more times than I can count. Once you start catching yourself before the crash, you realize most of your problems weren't the world's fault; they were just your first reactions getting too much attention. It can take you from "my boss is a dumbass," to "that dumbass made the best decision he could in the moment."

The Media Trap: Emotional Hijacking

Most people never reach that second reaction either. The media know it, and they feed on it. They bank on us reacting before thinking. Every headline is bait for your first emotion: anger, fear, outrage. That's their business model.

Outrage is profitable. Fear keeps you clicking. Division keeps you scrolling. Every headline, every "BREAKING" banner, every hot take is engineered to hijack your limbic system before your brain gets a vote.

I remember going into my 20s and starting to 'involve' myself in the world around me by signing up for notifications from my local news network. It took only a month for me to decide to shut it down. Every day, multiple times, I'd get these news alerts, and they would be about something negative. This person died, that person is suing, this place is shutting down, some candidate is catching shit for what they said. Maybe one in 20 headlines ever made me smile.

That was just local news. Then you add national networks, political outlets, influencers, and comment sections, and suddenly your brain's living on a diet of negativity and outrage. The more emotional you get, the more valuable you become.

They know you'll react faster to something that makes you angry than to something that makes you think. That's why headlines rarely aim to inform anymore; they seek to ignite. They aren't written to be accurate; they're written to make you feel something strong enough to share before you even read the article.

And the truth is, they don't even need to lie. They just need to frame. A few choice words, a cropped clip, and they can steer public opinion like a joystick. They don't show you reality; they show you the reaction that keeps you online.

But it's not just "the media." It's the algorithm. It's every post that rewards engagement over truth. It's creators who weaponize empathy for clout, and audiences who treat emotional outrage like a hobby. You don't just consume the chaos, you forward it, comment on it, repost it, keep it alive. You become part of the marketing team for your own manipulation.

A perfect example of how easily we can be led to feel before we think, and how the media takes full advantage of that, was the 2025 aviation landscape. In just the first half of the year, we saw four high-profile aircraft crashes that dominated headlines:

January 29 – Potomac Midair Collision: A CRJ-700 collided with a military Black Hawk over Washington, D.C., killing all 67 people aboard both aircraft

Two days later, a medevac Learjet crashes in Pennsylvania. Eight more dead.

Mid-February — A Delta Connection jet overruns a snowy runway in Montreal. Fifty-four onboard. Twenty-one hurt.

April — A sightseeing helicopter breaks apart midair over the Hudson River. Six fatalities. A family of five among them.

For two months straight, every time you opened your phone, there was another headline, another fireball, another "exclusive eyewitness." The story the media built was simple:

aviation was collapsing. Flying had suddenly become dangerous again.

"Why are so many planes crashing?"

"I fly tomorrow, and it seems so unsafe to fly this year."

"What's going on in the aviation world? It has to be the 5G."

But here's the truth: Statistically, Aviation safety in 2025 has still been strong overall, regardless of the handful of incidents that dominated the headlines.

Even with a late-year government shutdown that jammed up airspace and slowed operations nationwide, the safety records hold steady.

The difference weren't in the numbers; they were in the spotlight. These weren't just routine incidents that get passed off and receive no more publicity than local news. They were high-profile. Civilian jets. Military cross-traffic. Foreign tourists. Crashes near major cities. Perfect fuel for a media frenzy.

This is what happens when emotion drives before facts do. A few tragedies become the story of an entire industry, and suddenly everyone's panicking about a problem that doesn't exist.

Comfort, Compassion, and Cowardice

Being an adult involves managing your own emotions. The world doesn't need more people who explode or hide every time they're uncomfortable. But that's precisely what so many do; they confuse comfort for peace.

Think about a time you felt stuck or stagnant at your job, in your relationship, your hobbies, or your sport. Was it because it wasn't moving or growing? Or was it you? How often did you choose not to take on extra responsibility and learn a new skill at work? Or maybe not communicating with your partner and having that "I'm getting bored" conversation? You stayed quiet instead of having the hard talk. You coasted because trying again meant risking failure.

Maybe you play a sport or have a hobby in which you have learned what you could at your skill level, but you've been avoiding the hard path to learn a new skill because you don't want to fail. You are finally feeling confident. Why would you ruin that?

The best growth in your life will never come from comfort, and you already know that. Your brain knows it. You've heard it your whole life. But when your feelings whisper 'stay safe,' you still listen. That's the problem.

Comfort isn't the only disguise emotion wears. Sometimes it shows up dressed as compassion, and that's where things get messy.

We tell ourselves we're being kind, but often we're just avoiding discomfort. We don't want the awkward conversation, the conflict, the risk of being the 'bad guy.' But hiding behind kindness is still cowardice.

Just as staying within our comfort zone can halt our own growth, it can also harm someone else's, as well as the relationship between the two of you. We can't expect others to improve if we don't let them know where there's room for improvement, especially for those in leadership roles. Being "nice" is not the same thing as being honest, and often enough, helping someone means calling them out, not coddling them.

Now, this isn't a leadership course; there are plenty of resources out there for that, but one of the foundations of being a leader is to have your shit in check. Leadership demands emotional intelligence. Acting upon your feelings more often than not creates a chasm between you and your team, and it typically takes everybody to come together and fix it. And the larger the team, the harder that gets.

However, this doesn't have to be limited to leader-to-team member interactions; it can also be friend-to-friend, husband-and-wife, or mother-and-son relationships. Avoiding confrontation because it feels mean can actually cause more harm in the long term, as protecting yourself from discomfort often prevents both you and the other person from growth.

This isn't just about bosses and teams. It's about anyone who has to hold someone accountable, whether it's a friend to friend, a partner to partner, or a parent to a child. Avoiding confrontation doesn't make you friendly; it makes you dishonest. Real compassion tells the truth, even when it stings.

When you dodge hard conversations, you're not sparing someone—you're abandoning them. You're choosing your comfort over their growth. Problems you avoid don't disappear; they ferment. What starts as a small misalignment can turn into dysfunction, resentment, and ultimately collapse.

Leadership and Consequences

Most people don't blow things up on purpose; they just stay quiet long enough for them to collapse on their own. That's what emotional avoidance does: it rots what you're too afraid to confront.

Sarah noticed that the hard way with one of her team members, Jake.

A few months back, Sarah started noticing Jake slipping. First, it was small stuff, being late to meetings, missing little deadlines, needing reminders for things he used to handle without thinking. Nothing huge, but enough to set off that gut feeling that something was off.

There was always a reason, too. A rough night, a bad client, and "I'm not feeling creative." Excuse after excuse.

Sarah knew it couldn't keep going like this. Still, instead of addressing it, she took the less confrontational approach by making jokes, little jabs, sarcastic nudges, hoping he'd take the hint.

Fast forward six months, and Jake's not just slipping anymore; he's sliding. And he's taking the team with him.

He's now borderline insubordinate, openly resisting feedback, refusing to take ownership of his mistakes, and still relying on emotional excuses for professional failures.

The team has taken notice as well. They've begun to no longer take her leadership or word seriously anymore. Her lack of management over Jake has shown that they no longer need to give top-notch effort, either. They've even started to absorb his toxic ways of thinking and are now becoming harder to manage.

Sarah knows she can't ignore it anymore. But now? Now it's not one conversation, it's a backlog.

Calling Jake out today means admitting she let things slide for months. That she saw it and said nothing. That she enabled it. If she confronts him now, it's not just about his behavior; it's about her credibility. And he knows it. If she speaks up now, he'll say, "Why didn't you say anything before?"

"You never had a problem with it before."

"You're just changing the rules on me now."

And he's not entirely wrong. That's the cost of silence. The longer you avoid the discomfort, the bigger it gets. A conversation that could've taken 10 minutes with some awkward tension is now a full-on intervention with one person, and a whole team backing him up.

Avoiding confrontation isn't just giving comfort; it's building a trap.

Now, Sarah isn't just fighting Jake's attitude; she's fighting the monster her silence built. Every day she didn't speak up added another brick to it. What started as one uncomfortable conversation is now a wall between them.

Maybe you've been biting your tongue with a friend who keeps crossing lines, waiting for them to magically "get it." You think you're keeping the peace, but really you're keeping score.

Or it's your relationship. You keep dodging the hard talk about what's been bothering you because you don't want the argument. You tell yourself you're being patient, but really you're being passive.

It could be with yourself. You've been putting off the gym, the budget, the boundary, whatever it is, convincing yourself you'll get serious when the timing's right. However, the truth is that you're waiting to feel like it, and feelings don't owe you motivation.

Avoiding confrontation doesn't make life easier. It only makes the consequences louder when they finally arrive.

You're not wrong for having feelings. You're wrong for letting them run the damn show. Every time you let your emotions dictate your actions, you trade long-term progress for short-term comfort. Kick your feelings from the table because they don't get a vote. Your standards, discipline, and experiences do.

Next time your feelings step up to the mic, hear them out.

Then kindly tell them to sit the fuck back down.

- ϕ Emotional control is the muscle that separates how you feel from what you do.
- ϕ Your first reaction is instinct; your second is awareness; your third is choice. Train yourself to reach the third faster.
- ϕ Avoiding confrontation doesn't protect peace, it builds decay.

Excuses vs. Truths

Excuses	Truths
It's not worth the fight.	If it keeps bothering you, it's worth the conversation.
I don't want to hurt their feelings.	You're not protecting them, you're protecting your own comfort.
I didn't want to make things awkward.	Growth is supposed to feel awkward.
I didn't want to cause drama.	Avoiding honesty is how drama grows in silence.
I don't want to look like the bad guy.	Doing what's right rarely looks good at first.

Challenge Question

Where in your life are your emotions still running the show, deciding what you say, when you act, or what you avoid?

Excuses Built Your Prison

"I'm not built like that."

"I need motivation."

"I'm not a morning person."

"I don't have time."

"It's just not the right time."

"I'll start Monday."

Aren't you tired of lying to yourself and building this suffocating prison around you? You think you're free because you make your own choices. But you're not. You're shackled to the same tired stories you keep spoon-feeding down your throat and everyone's around you. Every excuse you defend is another brick in the prison you're building and another bar in the cell locking you in.

You're not stuck because of the world. You're stuck because you won't shut the fuck up and adapt to it.

You call it preference. You call it timing. You call it being realistic. But it's not realism, it's retreat dressed as logic. Every time you trade discipline for comfort, you tighten the bars. You feel safe because it's familiar.

I saved this as last for a reason, because excuses sit underneath every brutal truth we've faced so far. Every chapter you've read ties back here. Every failure, delay, and half-finished promise starts with an excuse. So, when you stare into the mirror, remember that what you're really looking at are the stories that have kept you comfortable. It's time to stop hiding behind them and get honest with yourself.

The Comfortable Lie

Excuses almost always disguise themselves and appear logical and comforting, often wearing plain clothes and speaking in reason. They feel safe, but their real purpose is to protect your fragile ego, not your future.

That safety? That's the disguise.

When I hear people say, "I can't do that because I'm not a morning person," what I'm actually hearing is that they are unwilling to change habits to support their morning responsibilities. They've mistaken comfort for biology. Morning productivity isn't genetic; it's a skill that can be trained. People often blame their body clocks but refuse to admit that it's just their routines that need adjustment. Stop snoozing half the morning away.

But when someone tells me that they prefer afternoons and evenings over mornings, that tells me that they actually understand themselves. They aren't making an excuse; they're conveying that they have adapted their life to the preferences that support their needs and means for success.

What we are seeing here is linguistic laziness as self-deception. It's a mental shortcut people use to make their behavior sound relatable and straightforward, even if it's not true.

"I hate my job." I'm bored, under-challenged, and stressed, but scared to risk something new.

"I'm just blunt." I don't filter myself because it's easier to call rudeness honesty.

"I can't lose weight." I haven't stuck to one plan long enough to see results.

"I'm not tech-savvy." I've never taken the time to learn the tools I rely on.

"I'm just bad with money." I don't track the money I spend.

This laziness in our words isn't always hiding poor actions, but they are excuses nonetheless. We use them to wrap ourselves in a protective blanket of relatability—excuses dressed as honesty. It's easier to have a fun conversation with your coworker in the seat next to you and say, "This job sucks," instead of having an honest discussion about how it's no longer fulfilling your needs.

Your excuses are nothing more than mental junk food. Tasting good in the moment, the excuses make you feel better temporarily. They go down easy but leave you starving later. And in the long term, they erode your confidence and ambition. You don't get stronger by feeding yourself bullshit and dodging the hard thing. You're just reinforcing the exact life that you claim to hate and want to change.

It's not survival. It's sabotage. But you've told yourself this story so many times, you've started to believe it. You don't need another motivational video, speech, or quote. You need to face what lies beneath the excuses.

Identity as the Enemy

Many people are unaware that their excuses stem from the image they have of themselves. And you'll often fight harder to defend your current identity instead of building a new one. And it's that very identity you're protecting that is holding you back.

Do you ever use the phrase, "That's just how I am," or "I'm just not built for this?" Both put a ceiling above your head, a death sentence for growth. Think back. When someone told you that you can't or couldn't do something because of some made-up reason, how motivated were you to prove them wrong?

You aren't going to let some stranger put a limit on your abilities, right? Then why the hell are you doing it to yourself?

You're standing behind a locked door when you're the one with the key.

It's the manager who says, "I'm not creative," but consistently devises ways to keep the team motivated every week.

The guy in the gym who swears, "I'm not built for cardio."

The person everyone gets along with but claims, "I'm an introvert with crippling social anxiety."

The CEO who thinks, "I'm not a good leader," while everyone looks to them for direction.

The warehouse guy who limits himself by saying, "I'm not that smart," but at home can rebuild a whole engine blindfolded.

You aren't born lazy, anxious, or unmotivated. You weren't born with this maximum limit that you could never go beyond. You've just gotten really good at putting those limitations on yourself. When you tell people that "you need coffee to function" or "I'm just introverted," you're not being honest. You're building a character within yourself that avoids change for the sake of comfort.

And after a while, that character starts making your decisions for you.

You'll tell yourself what you want. You'll even say it out loud.

"I want to be fit."

"I want to do that hobby."

"I want to be a part of that group."

But when you follow it up with excuses like, "That's just not how or who I am" and "I'm just not motivated lately," you think these words are protecting you from the discomfort of exploration, failure, and growth. You're not protecting yourself from pain; you're defending laziness, procrastination, and a lack of discipline.

You can love yourself and still strive for more. In fact, holding yourself accountable and not giving in to your pitiful excuses is one of the best ways to show self-respect. Don't listen to the critics who treat accountability as if it's toxic, as if wanting to better yourself means you hate who you are.

Real self-respect means calling yourself out, not because you are broken, but because you are capable of more. Holding on to your excuses and flaws as if they are part of your identity isn't real growth; it's emotional hoarding. You're going to drown in it.

The Psychology of Sabotage

There are those around you who won't even try to pull you out of your downward spiral; they'll cheer you on all the way to the bottom. We live in a society where "taking a break" and "treating yourself" gets you a pat on the back for "prioritizing your mental health." When in fact, you are doing more damage by being rewarded because you showed up to work today, even though you were a little tired.

This isn't to say that pauses and breaks aren't important. Mental resets and time off are essential components of healing and growth. It just becomes a problem when the pauses become the performances.

Approval is not the same as accountability, and your craving for validation should not overshadow the joy of victory. Just because someone tells you "you're doing your best" doesn't mean you shouldn't admit to yourself that you can do better. That's called self-handicapping.

This could look like you posting your 'barely made it to the gym' selfie for applause instead of progress. Or constantly complaining about PTO not getting approved, yet you never pick up overtime to help others get theirs approved.

This isn't just my opinion, either; there's real psychology behind it. In 2012, a group of researchers—Hirt, McCrea, and Kimble—published a study in the Journal of Personality and Social Psychology that dug deep into a behavior we all recognize but rarely admit: self-handicapping.

It's when you create an excuse before the outcome is even decided. You could sabotage yourself by staying out drinking the night before a big day, skipping your prep work, or intentionally procrastinating. Then you try to gain sympathy or a cop-out for poor performance by prefacing it with, "I didn't get much sleep." Or maybe it's more subtle. You brag about winging it to show confidence when you are really just hiding your avoidance of preparation. Both are forms of self-handicapping. Both are ways to shield your ego, so if you fail, you've got a fallback. "I wasn't really trying" becomes the soft landing for not measuring up.

A few years ago, I fell victim to this after interviewing for a different role within the company. Leading up to the interview, I had learned more about the position, and the narrative was building that it was not a role that I would enjoy. I went into that interview with no prep and low motivation. I was, however, fueled with an ego driven by the stories I was telling myself. I was qualified for the role, and up to that point, I had always been offered a position after every job interview I had attended, with nearly 12 years of work experience.

I did not get the job.

I remember sitting there thinking, "It's fine, I didn't really want the job anyway." That's what I would also tell those around me. I'd say to myself that because I no longer "wanted" the position, I must've made it apparent in the interview somehow. In reality, I didn't prepare. I didn't go into that interview feeling underqualified, as if I had something to prove. I failed the interview, I caused that blow to my own self-esteem, and I covered it up by giving some bullshit "I just wasn't feeling it" excuse.

And you've probably done something like this too. You've bombed the thing you half-assed and then blamed it on the part of you that cared the least.

But according to the study, this short-term comfort comes with a long-term cost. People who self-handicap experience lower performance, higher anxiety, and reduced motivation over time. Even when they successfully deflected judgment, they still paid the internal price: self-doubt, guilt, and lost momentum.

Worse still, the research highlighted how society enables it. People respond with sympathy, not challenge. They validate your excuses instead of holding you to a higher standard. That makes self-handicapping socially accepted and dangerously easy to repeat.

This isn't just bad behavior. It's a pattern of self-sabotage dressed up as caution. And every time you do it, you reinforce the idea that protecting your ego matters more than chasing your potential.

Post about burnout online and you'll get a hundred 'same here' comments before you get someone who either asks what you're doing about it or provides useful solutions.

Real strength comes from showing up without the safety net. No disclaimers. No pre-fail excuses. Just raw effort and full accountability.

Burn the backup plan. Bet on yourself. Or keep rehearsing failure in advance.

Consequences and the Mirror

This is what self-sabotage looks like when it finally cashes its check.

I saw this tow truck driver on TikTok. He records every repo, and without fail, every single person has an excuse.

"I paid it!"

"You've got the wrong car!"

"But I have kids!"

They yell, they cry, they plead. One man screamed that he had only missed two payments and that he had a family to feed. Another said he mailed the check, but it must've gotten lost. Doesn't matter. The car's still being hooked, and they're still blaming the driver, as if it's his fault. It's the same energy as blaming the scale, the boss, or the world. Anything but the reflection.

And in nearly every instance, the repo spotter always finds them out and about shopping at places they absolutely have no place being while their car is past due. Old Navy, Sephora, or some sit-down restaurant.

You know what I love most about these videos is the glaring blindness every one of these individuals has to their own actions. Maybe a few of them just accept it for what it is, and we don't see that because it wouldn't make for good entertainment. It's funny until you realize you've done the same thing in quieter ways. But for people to seriously act like they do nothing wrong, blaming the driver, calling him names, acting as if he's the bad guy because they won't be able to get to work tomorrow, they are living and breathing the phrase, "fuck around and find out."

That repo is the real-life consequence of all the stories you've been telling yourself. And now your family, your kids, your job... they're all suffering from your lack of accountability. Life is like the repo guy—it doesn't care about your story; it's there to collect.

You feel like everything is fine while you delay the hard decisions. Life isn't listening to your intentions; it's reaping the benefits of your results. And when it does, it's never clean. It's messy, loud, public, and painful.

Look, at some point, you have to admit the problem isn't your circumstances; it's your tolerance for your own excuses. You've lived with them so long that they've become part of your personality. They've become your scripts. Your habits. Just "who you are."

But if you're being honest, you know damn well none of it's working. The routines you cling to are keeping you stuck. The stories you tell yourself don't lead anywhere. You're not progressing, you're recycling.

And the longer you recycle the same story, the duller it gets, until you forget you're even the one telling it.

You've built your life around avoidance. Around comfort. Around not being the bad guy in your own narrative. And maybe it worked for a while. Perhaps you convinced a few people. Hell, you've obviously convinced yourself.

But now you're here. Reading this. Feeling that little tension in your chest because part of you knows I'm right. You're not waiting for the right moment. You're waiting to not feel scared. Or tired. Or uncertain. But that moment doesn't come. You just get better at explaining why it isn't happening yet.

So here it is, plain and simple:

If you want out of the mess you're in, stop making excuses for why you're still in it. That's it.

You already know what needs to change. You've always known.

The question is whether you'll finally stop talking around it and do something about it.

You've built your own cage, but the door's been open the whole time.

Every excuse you've made just got torn down. Good. You needed the demolition.

Part Three isn't about feeling better, it's about rebuilding stronger.

The walls you hid behind are gone. Now let's build something that can actually stand.

- φ Every excuse is a brick in the prison you're building to protect your ego.
- φ Lazy language turns preferences into permanent limits.
- φ Real self-respect isn't self-love without standards; it's accountability without excuses.

Excuses vs. Truths

Excuses	Truths
I tried, but it didn't work.	You stopped when it got uncomfortable.
That's just who I am.	No, that's just who you've decided to stay.
I can't help it.	You can help it, you just won't.
That's just my personality.	That's your comfort zone talking.
I've tried everything.	You've tried everything easy.

Challenge Questions

Where are you still rehearsing failure in advance, cushioning the fall with excuses instead of climbing out?

PART 3:
REBUILD THE FOUNDATION

You Don't Need Balance or Motivation

Life's harmony comes from balance in both spirit and mind. Body and soul. When your masculine sun aligns with your feminine moon. Or whatever the hell Yogi man-bun 'Bodhi' posted to Instagram this morning. Balance sounds noble, but it's usually just a prettier way of saying 'I'll start when life's easier.' The truth is, balance requires the same work, effort, and growth that people keep avoiding—the very things necessary to improve their lives.

Where could you have been if you just jumped into it? Each one of these says, "I need the world to perfectly arrange itself before I take responsibility."

How many times have you told yourself you'll start when life's less chaotic? 'When I'm not traveling.' 'When I'm less stressed.' 'When things calm down.' Balance becomes the excuse that keeps you stuck.

Say it out loud and it sounds pathetic, doesn't it? But you've said it. I've said it. Everyone has. As we mentioned earlier, we are often our own worst negotiators when it comes to our wants and needs. That's how you end up talking yourself out of the very life you say you want. How do we get ahead of it? By recognizing it when it's happening, whether it's you, a coworker, or even a loved one.

How about these?

"I'll hit the gym when I feel motivated."

"I'll do my writing when I'm in the right headspace."

"I'll reach out when I feel like it."

"I'll quit smoking when I'm less stressed."

Then there's motivation, balance's twin illusion. The thing that gets you moving for five minutes, then ghosts you when it's inconvenient. It once made me think I could successfully run a custom T-shirt business. Six months later, only two dozen sales, and now… I'm writing a book instead.

It's a phenomenon that can get a well-fed dude like myself to strap on some runners and get out there in a false sense of reality that I'm some kind of marathon runner. Where's the motivation after the first mile? Flat on its face half a mile back.

Balance and motivation are tools that can help you overcome tough obstacles and get moving. But they're not infinite. Your balance topples and your motivation tanks the moment shit gets hard. People treat them like foundations when they're barely even crutches. So why do people hang on so tightly to these?

The Balance Myth

Balance is a magic we sell to ourselves as the equilibrium we need before we can start our growth, but in reality, it's a moving target that never shows up. No matter how much balance you try to find, you'll tip the scales in another direction or use it as a disguise for procrastination.

You don't need life to even out; you need to stop waiting for it.

It's the false prerequisite that we use to buy ourselves more time to act like the same comfortable shitbag we've become accustomed to. A noble way to tell people you're chasing change while making sure you never have to.

You don't admit it outright, you dress it up like patience.

"I'll start once the work slows down."

"When the kid's schedule eases up, I'll…."

"If the stress fades, I'll focus on myself."

Every one of these says the same thing: *I'll act when it's easy.*

It's a stalling tactic and bullshit reasoning that we use to avoid the hard things until everything is "even." But that's not how life works. Everything in life has weight to it, and some things just weigh more than others.

121

Own Your Sh*t: You're the Problem

It's not about balance. It's about priorities.

A single mother with two jobs doesn't doom-scroll herself calm before feeding her kids. A hockey player doesn't tell his coach he'll go back in when his heart rate settles. A parent doesn't wait for 'balance' before rushing a sick kid to the ER. When the stakes are high, no one waits; they act.

But that's easier in the moment. When the stakes are high, a kid's sick, or a jet is on final, you don't wait. You move.

Contrast that with "low-stakes" stuff like cleaning, working out, starting your business, or starting that project you've talked about for a year. The penalty doesn't feel urgent, and the consequences of *not acting* are delayed, invisible, or quiet. You get away with not doing it.

The dangers are hidden, though.

You skipped the gym and dieting until work slowed down. Work's busier now, and you're fatter and feeling worse about yourself.

You delayed your side hustle. Another year wasted in a job you hate, complaining about your schedule for the umpteenth time.

Ignored marriage problems because you believed they stemmed from an unbalanced life. Now you're divorced.

You've had the budget room to save money for health expenses, but you chose to spend money to help relieve work stress. But now you're sick and can't afford your down payment.

You called it waiting for balance, but really, you were just choosing comfort over consequence.

You keep waiting for balance, not realizing it's never been real. Life isn't math; it's weight, and you decide what gets heavy.

Balance Is Perception, Not Reality

Is the *balance* we are looking for simple math?

- 8 Hours of sleep

- 8 Hours of work

- 8 Hours of free time

Perfect on paper, but life isn't a spreadsheet. It takes the slightest nudge to knock it over. Bills need to be paid, people get sick, and deadlines get pinched. Suddenly, those "equal buckets" no longer exist.

Balance looks clean in theory, until real life starts smudging the math.

In the year 2000, Sue Campbell Clark published an interesting theoretical paper in Human Relations (a management/psychology journal). It was known as the Work-Family Border Theory.

Clark's idea was that people manage internal "borders" between things like life, school, work, family, etc. Using studies on stress, satisfaction, and role conflict, she built the case that our satisfaction with *balance* is *perceived* as needing to be equal parts, but is *felt* by how flexible, strong, and clear those parts are, especially in terms of the amount of control people have over them.

She believed that people feel more balanced when they feel in control of their boundaries, such as how much time they spend working after hours and at home, or how much family time they get compared to time with their friends.

These borders and trade-offs are not equal slices of the same pie. You can work 60 hours a week and feel fine if your lines are drawn and you know where they are. Work 25 hours with no boundaries and you'll still feel wrecked.

When your borders align with your needs and priorities, you experience more satisfaction and less conflict. However, when they don't, things bleed over into other areas, and that's when you feel "out of balance."

Before I even found Clark's theory, I had already been experiencing a clear example of her work. Throughout my working career, I have pretty much always been someone who put in way more time and effort than what was expected of me, for better or worse.

As I have found purchase in my current career, my workaholic tendencies that I've always had have not slowed. If anything, they have grown as I've reaped the rewards of my hard work and dedication. Hell, so far, one of my most prized possessions is a simple Challenge Coin that one of my upper managers gave to me in recognition after an ass-busting weekend.

Own Your Sh*t: You're the Problem

I'll hear people give me shit to stop working after I've clocked out and gone home. Or they'll scoff when they see me in the office for a one-hour meeting on my day off. Or even the occasional "try-hard" because I've worked on a side project on my own time to not eat into my regular day-to-day duties.

I've never complained about my work-life balance. Something I've said in nearly every instance.

I used to wonder if they were right, if I was overdoing it. However, I never felt unbalanced; I was just driven. Work "invades" my life only as much as I allow it to. Never more.

Every off-day meeting or self-induced project I've worked on behind the scenes has been within my boundaries, while also comfortably balancing my family and other endeavors.

Life isn't balanced. Some things weigh more than others. It's not splitting your life into neat little buckets. It's border, trade-offs, and priorities. When you know where those lines are, you can feel steady even when life is lopsided. When you don't, you'll feel wrecked no matter how light your load really is. That's the truth. Balance is perception, not reality. And once you stop hiding behind the illusion of balance, you see how much of your life you've been delaying. But balance isn't the only lie. If balance keeps you waiting, motivation keeps you bouncing between action and failure.

The Motivation Trap

Motivation isn't a foundation; it's a feeling. It can spark movement, but it can't sustain it. It's emotional caffeine, good for a jolt, but useless for endurance.

Motivation will make you a starter, not a finisher. It's inconsistent: up at 8 a.m. and gone by lunch. It gets you out of bed to work out, but once you're sore, tired, or distracted, it's nowhere to be found.

How often have you listened to an inspirational YouTube video or motivational podcast or heard some super-clever life quote? I'm guessing you've felt that fire under your ass that got you into a headspace to get things done.

The spark is real, the staying power isn't.

Positive motivation can start something, but negative motivation hits harder. It's that guilt-fueled burst that shows up only after you've screwed up. It's reaction, not intention.

You screw up, get in a fight with your partner, and suddenly you're motivated to plan date nights. A week later, you're back to your old habits.

The doctor tells you that your blood pressure is through the roof. Now you're getting serious about the gym. A few weeks later, the membership was canceled.

You go into a negative balance in your bank account, so you cut all spending to save. After stress, boredom, and shitty groceries, you crash and take an overly priced vacation.

Most people don't change until the pain outweighs the comfort, then they quit as soon as the comfort returns.

Many people don't get motivated until they are in a difficult situation. They get the energy to start climbing the ladder, but get tired by the fourth rung and just sit back down.

I read an analogy once that motivation was like lighter fluid. Once lit, it burns bright but fast. Unless there is something more solid to sustain the fire, it'll go out.

When I joined my first hockey team in 2024, I couldn't afford a custom jersey, so I bought a cheap heat press and made one myself. That little project snowballed into an Etsy shop called G-Shirts.

Excited by it, I began experimenting with other designs and shirts. This very quickly turned into an "I can turn this into a side hustle" kind of idea. And it did. I had a Jeep hoodie design that was quite popular through Christmas, but it was taken down due to copyright issues that I didn't understand. By April, sales were dead, and I was no longer enjoying it or making cash. So, I shut down the Etsy shop and now do word-of-mouth work.

The second the novelty and cash dried up, so did my drive, because it was never a passion or discipline, just dopamine.

That's motivation in a nutshell, a sugar rush that feels like change until the crash hits. If you don't build something sturdier underneath it, you'll keep mistaking the spark for the fire.

Motivation burns out fast. So how do you keep the fire going? That's the part everyone misses, keeping it alive after the spark.

Psychologists Deci and Ryan dug into this decades ago and found that it isn't about getting more hyped, it's about why you're doing it in the first place. They split it into two ways: you're either acting because something's pushing you (extrinsic), or because it matters to you (intrinsic).

Sounds simple, right? But even the good kind, the stuff you actually care about, still collapses unless three things are in place: you feel like it's your choice (autonomy), you feel like you can actually do it and see progress (competence), and you've got people in it with you (relatedness). Miss one of those, and your motivation tanks. That's why relying on motivation is suicide. It's fragile as hell. Structure and standards carry you when motivation disappears, and it always disappears.

Foundations Need Structure

Balance keeps you from starting. Motivation keeps you from finishing. One tells you to wait until life is calm, the other tells you to move only when you feel like it. Both can sound noble. Both can feel good in the moment. And both can keep you spinning in the same damn spot.

You don't need balance. You don't need motivation. You need something sturdier. Structure. Standards. Systems. The kind of foundation that holds when shit gets heavy and doesn't collapse the second your feelings shift.

This next part of the book is where we pour concrete. You've torn down the excuses. Now we lay the framework, habits, boundaries, and standards that won't budge, no matter what storms come our way. From here on out, we're not talking about balance or motivation. We're building the damn foundation.

- φ Balance is a disguise for procrastination. You're not waiting for things to even out, you're waiting to feel comfortable enough to start.
- φ Motivation is a sugar rush. It'll get you moving, but it won't keep you there once it wears off.
- φ Control beats emotion, and structure beats motivation. The second you rely on how you feel, you've already lost consistency.

Excuses vs. Truths

Excuses	Truths
I just need to find balance first.	Balance isn't found; it's built through priorities and boundaries.
I'll start when life settles down.	Life doesn't settle; you do.
I've been waiting for motivation.	Motivation is the child of movement, not the parent.
I just can't stay motivated.	You're hooked on excitement, not consistency.
I'll do it when I feel ready.	Readiness is built, not felt.

Challenge Question

In what areas of your life are you still waiting for balance or motivation to show up before you move?

Raise Your Standards

"A chain is only as strong as its weakest link."

"A team is only as good as its worst player."

"You're only as good as your last performance."

"You're only as kind as the help you give when no one's watching."

I'm sure you've heard these or something like them many times before. Why? Because they are effective, tailorable, and relatable. But what do all these have in common? They all expose how low your bar is.

Standards.

They shape your identity, reputation, habits, and trustworthiness. The standards you set for yourself not only create consistency and trust you have with yourself, but they also shape how you are perceived by those around you.

We aren't talking about the super CEO or life coach guru shit like, "I don't go to a meeting unless I've visualized the outcome for 10 minutes beforehand."

"I don't start my day without an ice bath, 20 minutes of meditation, and journaling three wins from yesterday."

"I don't buy anything unless it moves me toward my five-year vision."

We are talking about real, tangible standards. The 7 Brutal Truths should be the baseline behind YOUR standards. And they don't need to match anyone else's, they just need to hold when life punches you in the mouth.

You'll see this again when we discuss becoming the person you want to be by mirroring the things they do. In doing so, you'll find and hear their individual standards and values. While yours may sound the same on paper, they are unique to you, your morals, and your own life experiences. A simple example, you and a coworker might both "not allow toxic people to taint your mood." Still, your definitions or limits of toxicity will probably differ from theirs.

The point isn't to copy someone else's rulebook; it's to make sure yours don't fold the second life hits back.

The Slippery Slope of Good Enough

Our standards, or lack thereof, form over time from convenience, not capability. Think of it like the Law of Inertia. You know the line, "an object at rest stays at rest, and an object in motion stays in motion." Your standards will match your current momentum and will begin to fall into a lazy state if you don't challenge them.

What was once important to you can just become "good enough." That's how your standards slide, not in a crash, but a shrug.

For example, you once valued having a clean sink, but one week you let them pile up a bit. You eventually loaded the dishwasher, but took your time unloading it, allowing the dishes in the sink pile up again. It bothered you fairly quickly, so you got them all done at once.

A few days go by, and you find yourself in the same position again, but this time you let it go a day or two longer. The cycle repeats again.

A few more days or maybe weeks go by, and now you find yourself being okay with just washing the dishes only when you don't have any left. Now you've got a week or longer between each full dish-cleaning day. And when those days happen, you feel good, and the dishes are clean for the day. But they'll be dirty again next week. That's okay because you'll get to them again and have another nice dopamine hit.

Now you've built a standard that cleaning dishes only when none are left is okay. Who knows how long that habit and standard will last? It's your new norm.

That's how comfort disguises decay.

Here's the catch, though: fixing it sucks. Undoing a lazy standard takes time and effort, far more than keeping a firm one. Now comes the struggle of reforming your old habit of having a squeaky clean sink, when you could have challenged your standard from the beginning and not let it fall to the wayside.

Let's back it up. Let's say you do have that cleanliness standard, and you fall short of it for a day. Did you fail yourself? Personally, I think we are human, and in the right circumstances, some wobbles are healthy and okay. If you were to ask yourself, "Will I feel good if I leave these dishes? Or will I feel like I'm just skipping out?" Your answer dictates whether or not you get it done. If your standard says that those dishes need to be done, but you think to yourself, "I won't be upset," then you need to get them done.

This is where "good enough" sneaks its way in. You remember that douchebag inner voice we talked about earlier?

Yeah, it's the threat that will find you anywhere and anytime. It keeps you from feeling guilty when you actually should. Letting things slide when you know they shouldn't.

That's the voice that keeps you average. The one that tells you you've earned rest when you haven't. The second you listen, you trade progress for comfort.

Claimed vs. Actual Standards (The Detective Phase)

Now it's time to take a look at yourself and the standards you've been letting slide because real growth starts when you admit that your baseline is embarrassingly low.

Your "detective phase" begins with identifying what you actually do, versus what you claim you do. Some examples of these may include the following. Do any of them sound familiar? Maybe you or someone you know?

Claimed standard: *"I'm disciplined with my mornings."*

Actual Standard: You consider it a "win" because you don't wake up at the last minute like others; you have plenty of time every morning, as you get up on the first or second alarm. Yet you are still consistently late.

Claimed standard: *"I eat clean."*

Actual Standard: Eating whatever's easy and calling it 'balanced.'

Claimed standard: *"I'm always there for my friends or family"*

Actual Standard: Only when it's convenient or in your self-interests.

Claimed standard: *"I'm supportive of my partner's goals."*

Actual Standard: Offering verbal support without actually changing habits to support them.

Claimed standard: *"I'm an honest person."*

Actual Standard: You tell the truth, but only if it doesn't risk discomfort.

Claimed standard: *"I'm low drama / I hate drama."*

Actual Standard: You avoid direct conflict; however, you're okay with stirring the pot in rumors or gossip.

Claimed standard: *"I'm detail-oriented and thorough."*

Actual Standard: Only double-checking your work when the stakes are higher.

Claimed standard: *"I'm a team player."*

Actual Standard: You help when it's easy, but when it gets messy, you find some other task to 'help' the team.

That's the difference, one's the face you put on for people, the other's the bare minimum you settle for.

You'll want to spend the next week examining your questionable habits, actions, or conversations. Log them if necessary, especially when no one's around. Time and time again, we prove that what we do in the presence of others does not always show our true levels of discipline. Look for the areas where you know you did or said something that you didn't want to or knew you shouldn't have. The times when you betrayed a standard you set for yourself or need to set going forward.

So why do we let these get away from us? Most standards we live by begin somewhere, often with good intentions. So why the difference? A lot of times it's simply just perception. We want others to perceive us in a certain way, so we create a kind of "code" or "rule" that we live by. As if we are some kind of unmovable statue.

But most often, it's our autopilot decisions, made out of convenience, that cause us to waver between how we think we are and what we do. Fitting nicely into our Stop Negotiating With Yourself chapter, we see that convenience often trumps our goals. We may eat mostly healthy, but the times we don't are usually because it's easier to eat out for a day or two instead of going to the grocery store.

Maybe you are sitting in the office and you hear somebody talking negatively about one of your coworkers, even making fun of them. They ask for your opinion on the matter. Instead of adhering to your inner morals and standards, which dictate that you shouldn't gossip or fuel the drama, it's more convenient to go along with it. Negating them or trying to put a stop to it puts you in an uncomfortable place that you may not want to deal with. So you go along with it. You tell yourself it's harmless. But that's the moment you traded integrity for belonging.

In this case we are auditing the standard, "I don't like to gossip." Keeping in mind that we went against this out of convenience and comfort. The next thing we need to ask ourselves is, do we need to change our standards or our actions?

What You Do vs. What You Tolerate

We can separate those by asking "What do I do? And what do I tolerate?"

Most people judge themselves by their actions but ignore the fact that *what they tolerate* sets an equally powerful, and often lower, standard.

Your actions show the standards you live by. How you eat, work, train, spend, or show up. That's what makes you uniquely you.

What you tolerate are the behaviors in others that you allow them to pressure you with. The habits that you accept, excuse, or worse, absorb. Because we can't control other people, what you allow from them exposes the weakness of your own standards.

You say you value your health, you walk after dinner (your action). But you also let your friends pressure you into drinking every weekend (your allowance).

You can be punctual (in your actions). Still, suppose you keep tolerating late friends and shrugging it off (in your allowance). In that case, you're indirectly lowering your standard for time.

You can work hard (your action), but if you let a boss undervalue and underpay you (your allowance), your standard for self-worth is still low.

You can be the most productive (through your actions), but if you let coworkers dump their work on you without pushback (through your allowance), your standard for self-respect is weak.

People like to brag about their actions: "I only get Dunkin' Donuts coffee on the weekends." But their *tolerances* reveal the truth ("My boyfriend and I only cook dinner once a week, we eat out the rest.) That's the part people won't post, the proof that their standards collapse the second comfort shows up.

Your life isn't just shaped by what you do, it can ruined by what you let slide.

This is where the Tightening Your Inner Circle chapter will test you later. External pressures are often the most challenging aspect of resetting your standards. We are social animals at our core and are hardwired to act with the pack. If you are a social butterfly or a people pleaser, it will be important to stick to your guns against your friends and loved ones. You're doing this for you, not them.

Your life isn't just shaped by what you do, but what you let slide.

And once you stop letting things slide, the world's going to notice. Your circle will test you. Chances are that your coworkers, friends, and even family will all want the old version of you back. They'll call you distant, obsessive, "changed." Good, fuck them. You're not doing this for them. You're doing it for you.

The truth is, you don't raise your life by reaching higher; you start by refusing to sink lower.

Raising the Floor, Not the Ceiling

Here's where I believe most self-help books and those of super-disciplined CEOs and entrepreneurs get a little too "rah

rah rah." Everyone's fantasizing about the summits instead of spending little more attention to fixing the dirt they're standing on.

You can't reach the top of the mountain if you are still on your couch. You need to get to the base first and you start by raising the minimums.

Now don't go thinking this is me caressing your cheek and saying, "You go at your own speed, sweetie." No, I'm telling you your speed is irrelevant if your standard is crawling. If the floor you live on is pathetic, then it doesn't matter how high you think your ceiling is.

Stop fantasizing about the summit when you won't even lace up your boots. Raise the damn baseline. That's where progress starts.

A real standard is not some complicated, far-reaching goal that requires 150% effort to meet. It's repeatable and clear-cut. You won't have confidence in your own instruction manual if it is filled with new standards that have only a 20% success rate. If you want to know what real standards look like, not the ones you fantasize about, but the ones you can actually live by, here's the difference.

Intended Standard	Unreachable Target	Repeatable Action
I'm detail-oriented.	I'll never make a mistake again.	I reread every email before sending.
I'm always prepared.	I'll anticipate every question in the meeting.	I walk into every meeting with at least one question or idea.
I eat healthy.	I'll stick to a perfect diet with zero slip-ups.	I cook at least four dinners at home each week.
I use my time well.	I'll schedule every hour of my day and not waste a minute.	I limit mindless scrolling to 30 minutes a day.
I'm always there for my friends.	I'll keep in constant touch with everyone.	I check in with at least two people a week.
I stay positive.	I'll never feel depressed again.	I reframe my bad days before they ruin my mood.
I'm a supportive partner.	I never need to be asked, I know what my partner needs.	I make at least one daily gesture of support.

We communicate well.	We'll solve problems instantly and never argue.	We don't end an argument until we've listened.

Defining our standards takes time, and they evolve as our lives progress. What starts as "No TikTok scrolling for more than 30 minutes a day" can grow into "No TikTok on the weekdays." And may eventually turn into deleting the apps altogether. Therefore, it's essential to audit these regularly, every couple of weeks or months, to ensure you're progressing in the direction you want to go.

But none of this means shit if it only works on your best days. The real test comes when everything goes wrong, and that's where we're heading next.

Testing Your Standards Under Pressure

Now, these standards are only as good as they are under pressure. It's easy to cook food at home multiple times a week when the fridge is full. But what about when it's empty? Is the standard you set strong enough to get you to the grocery store after a stressful day at work, or will you give in easily and order out?

Look at that, you just negotiated with yourself again. See how easy it happens? And you'll justify it every time, too. That's how standards rot.

If your standards break easily, then they are just wishes. They've got to survive bad moods, bad days, and plain bad luck.

A personal standard for myself is *unrelenting approachability.* Let's say I'm at work; I could be in the worst mood or be buried in six different tasks all demanding my immediate attention. However, if one of my peers, colleagues, or bosses comes up and needs my attention, there will never be a moment when I make them feel belittled or like they can't ask me a question. I take enormous pride in being someone who people can count on to ask questions or seek assistance from without feeling like they may upset me or be a bother.

Does that mean I can handle everybody's concern at any moment? Drop what I'm doing to help them out or collaborate on a specific action item? No. That would be the Unreachable Target. Sometimes what I'm focused on needs my attention first. However, my Repeatable Action is to meet their need with either sincerity or a willingness to help. I may ask them, "Can this hold just a second?" or tell them, "If you can give me a few minutes, I'll be ready to help you out." Now, while these white-collar phrases may not be the exact words that come out of my mouth every time , the message, intent, and feelings are all the same. I'll say something to make the individual feel that while I am more than willing to help, I'm just currently tasked.

Now, how do I audit this? How do I know that I am meeting this standard? I see it in small ways every day. Often enough, I'll have a simple three-minute task take 30 minutes or longer to complete because I get sidetracked by questions or collaborations with other team members. If they weren't comfortable asking, they'd go somewhere else. Even when I'm off and not working, some of my coworkers are comfortable enough to text me to ask for help.

Believe it or not, this standard didn't come from leadership books; it came from embarrassment.

I believe this it began when I worked the front counter at our local McDonald's during high school.

I had just begun driving, and my buddies and I were talking about our cars. The topic of oil changes came up, and I had innocently mentioned that I didn't know how to change my car's oil. The immediate shit I got from all of them was cataclysmic.

"What do you mean you don't know how to change the oil? It's fucking easy!"

"No point in learning now, you'll break a nail."

Followed by many more insults that will get me cancelled if I repeat them.

You may call it luck, but I grew up in a household where we took our cars to a mechanic for all maintenance needs. Not once was I ever in a position to learn how to change the oil in a car. So how on earth would I know how to do this?

I remember this causing me to feel small and *less than* the other guys. While logically I knew that I probably had skills in things that they didn't, I still wasn't a fan of being shit on for not knowing something that up to that point, I had no reason to learn.

To this day, I still cringe when someone makes another person feel small for asking a question, seeking assistance, or simply not knowing something. We all live different experiences and are exposed to different things, so being approachable and letting someone ask questions without worrying about retribution is an unwavering standard of mine. The more people ask questions, the more we can all grow and learn from each other.

That's my standard. It's not perfect, it's not glamorous, but it's repeatable and it's mine. And that's the point, standards don't stick because you wish them to. They stick because you reinforce them.

Most people think standards run on good intentions, but they don't. Without reinforcement, they'll buckle under moods, stress, or laziness. That's why the next step isn't about chasing motivation or waiting for the right mindset. It's about building the systems, the unsexy guardrails, that make sure your standards fire every single day, no matter what mood you're in.

φ Standards are your real identity. They decide who you are when no one is around.
φ "Good enough" is the death of growth.
φ A real standard isn't perfect; it's repeatable.
φ Standards don't hold because you *want* them to, they hold because you reinforce them.

Excuses vs. Truths

Excuses	Truths
I already have high standards.	Then prove it on the days you don't feel like it.
At least I'm trying.	Trying is the first step, not the last.
I'm doing better than most people.	Comparison is a race to the bottom. Your bar shouldn't be measured against theirs, measure it against your potential.
I've improved a lot already.	Progress isn't a finish line.
I'm fine where I'm at.	"Fine" is failure in disguise.

Challenge Question

What's one low bar in your life that you've been pretending is "good enough?"

Build Systems, Not Vibes

You keep waiting to "feel ready." You keep telling yourself you'll get serious when life slows down, stress eases up, and when the vibes feel right. How are the vibes working out for you? Probably the same way it worked out for me in my twenties, broke, overweight, and scrambling. Motivation came and went. Progress crawled.

Balance was temporary, only ever showing itself after a payday. What finally worked wasn't a mood; it was *systems*.

Systems are the boring, repeatable, mechanical things that run while you're tired, stressed, pissed off, or distracted. They're a pre-decision. The choice that is made before the moment of weakness ever arrives. If your life runs on vibes, your moods are in charge. If your life runs on systems, you are.

You don't need to turn into a robot to stay consistent. It's about building structure so the stress of chaos hops off your shoulders, leaving you feeling alive. Structure doesn't cage you, it carries you. Discipline isn't a prison; it's peace. They keep the promises you made to yourself when you were clear-headed and serious, so you don't keep getting sabotaged by the version of you that's tired and lazy.

Vibes whisper, systems deliver.

But systems don't exist in a vacuum. They need something to serve, a standard. Without one, all you've built is motion without direction.

Systems Uphold Standards

Standards mean nothing if there's nothing to hold them up.

If standards are what's done or avoided, systems are how they get done. Think of most sports. The rules are the standards, and penalties or fouls are how they're upheld.

You don't need to reinvent your life here, you just need to bridge the gap.

Repeatable Action (Standard)	Method of Upholding (System)
I reread every email before sending.	Using an email plug-in to delay sent emails by 60 seconds so you never forget to reread it.
I cook at least four dinners at home each week.	Grocery shop every Sunday and meal plan for the week.

Repeatable Action (Standard)	Method of Upholding (System)
I limit mindless scrolling to 30 minutes a day.	Set app time limits and keep your phone charger across the room at night.
If I cancel, I reschedule.	Use your calendar to cancel and set a new date immediately.
We don't let an argument end without acknowledging each other's side.	An internal agreement between the two of you that before you unload your side or end the argument, you repeat their side out loud.

Standards tell you what you said you'd do. Systems make sure you do them.

They literally take decisions away from you. And that's how they should be designed, as pre-decisions. Remember the quote about how feelings cloud your judgment?

"Your first emotional reaction is often what you are conditioned to feel. Your second is what you actually feel. Your third is who you decide to be."

The same rule applies to your decisions.

When you leave decisions up to the moment, you're betting on your weakest self to show up strong. Systems remove that gambling. They make the call before the chaos starts.

Remember, your feelings don't get a vote. Your systems have already decided.

Reduce Decision, Reduce Chaos

You can build all the systems you want, but if your day is filled with a thousand tiny choices, they may still collapse under the weight of chaos.

Every time you ask, "What's for dinner?", "Should I do this now or later?" or "Did I remember to do that thing?", you're burning mental fuel that should go toward real work.

My wife and I made a surprisingly huge boon in our communication and organization when we simply downloaded a shared calendar app. We had the normal, "Hey, do you work this day?" Or "I told you that we had dinner plans with so-and-so!" But once we downloaded the app, we quickly found ourselves communicating more easily about scheduling things. I noticed that to-do lists were getting done faster and that we actually had more time available than I originally thought. It also helped ensure things weren't getting pushed off nearly as much. If I put "Haircut" on the calendar for a Tuesday when I'm off, the chance of me actually getting it done is much higher.

Less decisions, less thinking, more freedom.

A study by Baumeister in the late 1990s and early 2000s examined willpower and decision fatigue, as well as a phenomenon known as ego depletion. Simply put, they believe your willpower to be like a muscle. The more you use it, the more tired it gets. Each decision you make, no matter how small, pulls from the same limited mental energy battery.

In one study, people who resisted eating cookies quit faster on a difficult puzzle than those who gave in. Fighting temptation drained their willpower. The lesson? Every time you rely on willpower instead of a system, you're wasting energy on resistance instead of results.

Ever notice you buy more junk after a long day? That's decision fatigue. You spent all day deciding, so by 6 p.m., the only thing your brain can commit to is Doritos.

A real-world example is found in the judicial system and the parole process. Certain prisoners have the chance for parole during their sentence. These hearings are randomly assigned throughout the day, and decision fatigue has been attributed to a distinctive difference in how lucky a particular prisoner is. Prisoners assigned to an earlier hearing have proven to be far more likely to be granted parole than their counterparts scheduled for an afternoon hearing. After a few hours of decision-making, judges begin to tire and deny more requests. Being their default option, it's the easier choice.

Even as I write this, I catch myself getting lazy. Word choice starts slipping the longer I sit here. That's decision fatigue in real time.

"Oh, I'll revisit this in editing", I say to myself. Well, now I'm here in the editing phase, thinking to myself, "What the fuck was I writing here?"

What does any of this mean to us? It's simple: Reduce the amount of mundane decisions you make, and you'll have more capacity for the ones that need more attention.

Systems Build Freedom, Not Restriction

There's this common misconception that systems and rigidness reduce freedom. It makes us boring, stony, or takes away our "uniqueness." In fact, they actually give you more freedom, not restrictions. They aren't a prison and won't take away from the meaningful tasks and things in your life. They take care of the boring stuff, the menial things. Leaving you free to handle the other matters that you care more about. They ensure life runs smoothly while you live it.

Finances are an excellent example of this. I find that people don't budget for three reasons, or a combination of them. They're lazy, they don't know how, or they feel that a money system only tells them what them can't spend. But they're wrong with the last one. With a budget, you know exactly what you can spend guilt-free. Leaving the financial stress in the rearview. That's not restriction, that's control.

"But Niiiiiiiiiiiick, I have debt!" Cool. So do I. But you know what keeps me from stressing? By having a system that shows me that my bills can get paid and that I can only pay off my debt so fast without some extra hustling.

Here's how I built a system to eliminate paycheck-to-paycheck stress. These aren't my personal budget numbers, just the system I use to reduce the headache. For all you financial gurus out there who are bound to get bothered, well 👍. I'm still learning.

First off, my wife and I keep our personal finances separate. We work hard for our money and should get to do with it what we want, to a point. We have a house account with an agreed-upon amount that each of us are required to contribute to with each paycheck. This account covers all shared bills, including phones, insurance, rent, internet, and TV services, plus some additional funds to cover changes, bill spikes, or maintenance issues. We also have a joint savings account that we deposit money into with each check to save for our first house.

I personally have three individual accounts: a spending account, a bills/subscription account, and an emergency fund/savings. Each one has a job. That's what systems do: they assign every dollar a mission, so it never wanders off.

Now, each of these is pretty self-explanatory, but it's the distribution that has made my life simple to the point that I don't really need to stress about bills. Some of you may need to do things a little more manually, depending on your employer, but I'm able to have mine allocate specific amounts of each check into the individual accounts.

Because of this, my individual bills account is always funded, and everything that comes out of there is on autopay. The house and spending accounts also receive their allotted amounts, and any remaining funds are allocated to the emergency fund/savings account.

As long as I stick to my spending account and not dip into my savings unnecessarily, I have no stress about my bills. They are always paid on time and in full.

The system's not sexy, but neither is financial stress.

This system has also significantly helped my wife and I feel more financially secure together and eliminate any arguments about money. With the auto deposits and auto bill pays in place, as long as we don't blow our grocery budget, then everything is golden. Bills are paid, she has her money, and I have mine. If I make any decision that makes me broke, as long as I uphold my side of the house account, then it's my problem to deal with, not hers.

Systems don't make life smaller; they make it manageable. They don't kill freedom, they create it. Because when every critical part of your life runs on structure, you finally get to use your energy on what matters instead of constantly fixing what's broken.

And that's not just some "normal guy figured it out" lesson either. The best in the world live the same way.

Even the Best Have Systems

If systems sound too boring or mechanical for you, here's a reality check. The people operating at the absolute top don't leave anything to chance. They don't trust motivation. They trust mechanisms.

In an interview with Vanity Fair, President Obama said, "You'll see I wear only gray or blue suits, I'm trying to pare down decisions. I don't want to make decisions about what I'm eating or wearing. Because I have too many other decisions to make."

You can imagine that being President of the United States, decision fatigue is part of the job description. He's not trying to look iconic; he's trying to stay functional. Every shirt and tie already decided is one less ounce of decision fatigue weighing him down when real choices hit. And he's not alone.

Steve Jobs wore a black turtleneck, jeans, and sneakers every day to avoid trivial clothing decisions. Mark Zuckerberg did the same thing with a gray T-shirt and hoodie. They cared more about efficiency than style.

Even Jeff Bezos avoids decision fatigue by systemizing his schedule to leave big decisions for the mornings and reserve smaller decisions for later on. Bezos has his mornings carefully engineered for clarity, making big decisions early and small ones later. That's not randomness, that's rhythm.

Less surprisingly, world-class athletes do the same thing. Kobe Bryant outlined his systems in his book, *The Mamba Mentality*. His daily rituals included waking up at 4:00 a.m. every day to train twice before most people's first workout. He studied game film nightly, even down to his opponent's foot placement.

And Tom Brady? His entire career ran on routine. In *The TB12 Method*, he breaks down how he engineered his days around recovery, nutrition, and timing. He made sure the hardest decisions, the ones that demanded focus, happened early when his mind was fresh, and everything else ran on autopilot. It's the same principle Bezos follows, just played out on a field instead of a boardroom. Structure, not spontaneity, is what kept him performing at 45 like he was 25.

If that level of structure sounds obsessive, that's the point. Most people's days collapse under a pile of micro decisions: scroll or read, snooze or get up, cook or order out. These aren't harmless habits; they're tiny leaks that drain focus before anything meaningful happens.

Systems aren't meant to imprison you in monotony. They save you from the small things taking up precious brain power that you need to own your shit in other places.

The Slow Grind of Systems

But if they are so helpful, why don't we hear more about them?

Because they're slow, boring, sometimes fail, and don't always make the best television.

Those fad diets and 30-day challenges go crazy because committing for short periods is easy. They work, until they don't. Because as soon as the dopamine wears off, we are right back to eating Cheetos in our underwear.

Now you won't hear me totally shit on the XX-Day challenges like the "experts" will. Do they struggle to build long-standing habits? Yes. But they are fun, they get people moving in the right direction, and they challenge people nonetheless.

When I was doing my first round of 75Hard, I recall that I could feel the difference internally more than I could see it externally. I was taking my progress picture every single day, but couldn't see a damn thing changing. It was around day 40 that I compared my most recent picture to the one from day one. BAM! There it was. My tits were now a more respectable B cup. The results were there, even though I couldn't see them in the moment.

I have a friend who likes to use the phrase, "You can't see the forest from the trees." I love that saying because it's so simple and takes no effort to understand that perspective is everything. And vibes or feelings fuck with your perspectives.

That's why you track, not guess. Systems don't ask how you feel, they show you what's real.

"I don't feel like I've lost weight."

"I don't feel like my debt is any lower."

"It doesn't seem like I've gotten any better at [insert your subject]."

All these things compound and build until one day you get hit with the result. That number on the scale drops. You'll notice that the interest you're paying per statement is now half of what it was. You help a classmate answer a hard question that you once struggled with.

However, systems don't need to build towards only one thing. They can also prevent consequences. These are the most dull systems. Consider how you brush your teeth twice a day, wear your seatbelt, and go to the doctor for an annual checkup. Such menial things don't hold much weight because they don't produce results but rather prevent them.

You avoid thousands in dental bills, you don't die if you get in a car accident, or you avoid getting blindsided by something serious that your doctor has caught early.

You don't build systems because life's easy, you build them because shit will go wrong. And when it does, the grind is what saves you.

Systems Don't Have to Be Perfect

I'd bet a shit ton of money that at some point you've said, "If I'd started that thing months ago, life would be different." And the sad part? You probably still haven't started. That's another trap: waiting for perfection instead of starting with something messy.

Systems don't provide instant gratification; they offer permanent change.

Here's the real kicker. Systems don't have to be perfect. Standards should be sharp and uncompromising, but systems just need to be consistent. That's the beauty of them. A sloppy system that runs beats the perfect plan you never start. Perfection is just another excuse. Consistency is the win.

Perfection may appear productive, but it's often just procrastination disguised as clean lines and good intentions.

Every time you delay building a system, you're handing your life over to chaos. And chaos doesn't care about your excuses; it will bury you. The only way out is boring, repeatable, unsexy systems.

It doesn't argue, it just multiplies. Every undone system becomes another fire you'll have to put out later.

But even the best systems will collapse if the environment around them is working against you. You can't out-system a toxic setup. That's why the next step is building an environment that doesn't just support your systems, it makes them almost impossible to ignore.

You can't build discipline inside a dumpster fire. The best system in the world won't survive if everything around it pulls you backward.

So stop waiting for the vibe, the spark, or the right mood. Build the system. Stick to it long enough for it to actually fucking do something. Because if you won't own your systems, something else will: chaos, distraction, or the people who do.

- ϕ Systems are how standards stay alive.
- ϕ A sloppy system that runs beats the perfect one you never start.
- ϕ Chaos doesn't care about your feelings. Systems don't either.

Excuses vs. Truths

Excuses	Truths
I just need the right system before I start.	No, you need to start. Progress refines process.
My system keeps failing.	Either take a hard look at the system, your surroundings, or just do it until it does.
I don't have time to plan.	You're wasting more time winging it.
I like keeping things flexible.	Flexibility without structure equals chaos.
I'll get organized later.	Later is the landfill of potential.

Challenge Question

What system in your life have you been endlessly planning, instead of just running it messy and fixing it along the way?

Environment Eats Discipline

Everybody loves to say, "You just need more discipline." That's some of the laziest advice in the world. As if discipline is a light switch that can be flipped on and, boom, instant savagery. Seriously, if it were that easy, none of us would be fat, broke, or stuck in the same place or mindset we were five years ago.

Here's the truth: discipline, just like willpower, is not infinite. Research from Baumeister's study proved it just as true for our convictions and ability to stick to our goals, standards, and systems. Discipline is fuel, and you burn it all day long fighting temptations, distractions, choices, and whatever other bullshit you face.

Typically, people don't slam Oreos at 7 a.m. with their morning coffee. It's later in the day, after work or life was stressful and tiring, when you finally give in. It's not always because you suddenly don't care; it's because your tank is empty. It's not always weakness; it's just running on fumes.

This is where your environment wrecks you. If the Oreos aren't in your pantry, you never have to spend the last fumes of discipline trying to fight the urge to obliterate them. If your phone is charging across the room, you don't waste mental energy bargaining with yourself, "just five more minutes." Go the fuck to bed. Suppose your Amazon account doesn't have one-click checkout. In that case, you've given yourself one more barrier to rethink the purchase you're about to make. If you put your goddamn phone in another room, that's one less thing distracting you from getting the first draft of your freaking book done and not delaying it any further.

So I've heard.

Here's the brutal part. People know this. They just call it a discipline problem because it sounds noble. 'I need to be stronger' feels better than admitting you're sabotaging yourself.

Discipline burns out fast when you waste it on stupid battles you could've avoided. Protect it. Build an environment that fuels it, rather than feeding the fire. Because when the real fight shows up, you won't have shit left in the tank.

Everyday Environment

As we've discussed multiple times, seeing examples in others can help us recognize our own actions. So listen to those around you when they are talking about the habits, actions, and goals that they'd love to achieve but for "some reason" struggle. Odds are, you'll hear them saying something along the lines of, "I lack discipline," "I don't have time," or "I just can't stick to it." Then take a second to think about the things around them that are preventing it, but are in their control to change.

A lack of discipline isn't always to blame when you are setting yourself up for failure. Like when your pantry is stocked like a vending machine. If Little Debbies are staring you in the face every time you open the door and whisper sweet nothings in your ear, you're going to eat them. It's not necessarily a weakness when your environment literally puts a puppy on the table and dares you not to pet it.

The same goes for your fridge. Rows of ice-cold soda waiting for you to crack one open. But to get some water, you need to grab a glass, fill it, then throw some ice in. The soda, the sugar, the crispness, it's all right there, ready and convenient. Take it out of the fridge, and suddenly you find yourself drinking more water. Saving money and sugary calories too!

Even your grocery cart can betray you. Shop when you're hungry and without a plan, and you'll buy with your heart and stomach, not your brain. Remember what we said about feelings: they get an opinion, not a vote. Go in with a list, and you'll find that you budge far less and have fewer temptations at home.

How many times have you been driving and then stricken with a pang of hunger? You make the quick, easy decision to go through the nearby drive-thru to grab a quick bite to eat. If you keep a protein bar or two stashed in the glove box, you can satiate yourself until you get home, saving you time, money, and more calories.

And then there's the convenience of meal-prepping and prepacking your lunches. When you take the time to prepare the week's lunches, you don't even need to think about what you're going to eat. You've accounted for the calories, you're saving money, and you're relieved of the stress.

These tiny changes don't need to just affect your diet. Making environment tweaks can even help you meet your fitness goals.

When I was doing my second round of 75Hard, it was in the dead middle of winter. I was struggling more than usual to start my 4:30 a.m. outdoor workout because of all the extra clothes I had to put on. In the warmer months, it wasn't as much of a struggle. Open my eyes, throw on underwear, shorts, socks, shoes, and a shirt, then go. Come winter, you'll need to add extra layers, such as gloves, thermals, thicker socks, a beanie, nipple tassels, and possibly a face mask.

I had a few days where I swapped my workouts, or worse, did both in the evening, separated by a few hours, to align with the rules. This would have me going to bed late, which then affected my next morning and day. A classic domino effect derived from piss-poor time management.

My simple solution was something our parents taught us when we were young: setting out my outfit for the next day, the night before. I just took a few minutes to arrange my clothes where I got ready in the morning, stacked up in the exact order that I would put them on.

And there we were, back on track. Cold mornings still sucked, but a small hurdle was overcome by a simple

164

environmental change. No more walking from room to room looking for each piece of clothing in the morning while trying to avoid waking the wife.

If your bike's buried behind junk or your treadmill is doubling as a clothes rack, that's not just laziness, that's poor design. You made the hard thing harder.

However, environmental changes are not always simply about doing or not doing a task. Sometimes, these adaptations help you do things more effectively. How often while working out have you sat for longer than you should have, searching for the right music? Instead of being locked in, you're doom-scrolling on Spotify. Simply prearranging a playlist can help you stay in the game.

Every space you move through either fuels you or eats at you. Home, work, gym, car—they're all battlegrounds for your focus. The ones who keep winning aren't stronger; they just stopped letting their surroundings fight against them.

Workplace and Lifestyle Environment

"But Niiiiiiiiiiiick, home and gym life are easier to change. But at work, things are out of my control."

Oh yeah? Let's consider ways to improve our work life.

White-collar work often suffers from distractions at the desk that detract from your efficiency. For example, if you have two monitors at work but one is running Netflix all day, then you may need to rethink what's more important: your productivity or being caught up on your next brain rot.

You like the noise, and it helps you work? That's cool, good for you. I get it. I've dealt with pretty severe ADHD since I was a wee lad, but I grew up and learned how to recognize and overcome my own tendencies. I also like to multitask to help me focus on a singular thing, but I know that if my eyeballs can see it, I'll watch it. Put it on in the background.

Speaking of things catching your eyes, emails and messages love to pull your attention, and they're important… sometimes. Instead of catching them individually, you can turn off notifications and check them in batches.

Work from home? Set up a designated area solely for work. If the living room couch is your hangout spot, you're going to be more tempted to do those things while working as well. Even if it's in the same room, you can arrange the space a little differently to change the "feel" of the room.

My personal hack is that if I'm at home and having a severe distraction problem, I'll put on my socks and shoes. When I'm at home, I never wear them, regardless of whether I'm relaxing, working out, or just hanging with friends. So when I throw them on, I magically feel more prepared to do chores or focus. My brain flips to productivity mode.

Blue-collar workers don't tend to deal with distractions as much, since their work is less repetitive or has greater variance between tasks. Also, being in motion and using your body has proven to be an excellent distraction preventative.

What they do suffer from, though, is inefficiencies. Wasted time, messiness, and unpreparedness. When I was a cable guy, I religiously started or ended my day at a gas station. Having to stop between jobs to go get gas simply broke me out of the day's rhythm. I always preferred getting gas at night just in case I was running late in the morning. Back then, that was often the case, since I always waited till the last minute to roll out of bed. If I didn't get gas the night before, it was a guarantee that I would forget the next morning. We've all been on the shit end of that game.

Even your gear can slow you down. Do you only charge your batteries when they're empty? Cool, that may be right in the middle of the job. Unless you've got extra batteries ready, you're now sitting there with your thumb in your ass. You could set something up at home, in your truck, or at the shop to have the batteries charging between shifts or jobs.

And safety gear. Well, I've been on both sides of being a Safety Karen and OSHA's "evidence #1." One of the big differences between the safety standards was the accessibility of said safety equipment. The times when I and the teams I was on used our safety equipment were dictated by both company standards and whether or not that equipment was readily available.

Even a toolbox can play into how well a job goes. A put-together toolbox can help reduce time by making tools easier to find, harder to lose, and preventing them from becoming damaged.

But outside of the easy things like food, health, and work, how can we bring value to other aspects of our lives just by tweaking our environments a bit? You've probably already started putting together a theme and drawn some similarities with building systems or habits.

Want less screen time before bed? Charge your phone across the room. You can't doom scroll what you can't reach.

"But Niiiiiiiiiiick, I use my phone as my alarm, and and and what if there's an emergency phone call?"

They still make alarm clocks, Chelsea. You can even get one that matches your aesthetic if that helps you sleep better. Better yet, what if you have to actually get up to turn off the alarm? That'll get you out of bed faster.

Earlier, we talked about having 'one-click' set up with your Amazon account. Remove one-click. Better yet, remove saved cards entirely. Make yourself type the number every time. It's safer, and you'll think twice before buying.

Speaking of saving money, food-delivery apps, since COVID, have become a financial black hole. There are people out there who even take out small-time loans just to get a DoorDash delivery.

Delete the damn app. Out of sight, out of temptation, that's how you save both money and stress, not to mention unhealthy eating.

You can keep blaming burnout, motivation, or bad luck all you want, but check your setup. You've built the chaos you're drowning in. You stocked the fridge, you cluttered the workspace, you downloaded the distractions. So clean up your battlefield before crying about the war.

Quit Pretending This Is New

So, did you catch the overwhelming similarities between all these examples? Keeping protein bars in the car, having your bike within reach, filling the tank before work, laying out clothes, and keeping a clean toolbox; they're all the same move.

Written to-do list vs. memory.

Phone at the dinner table vs. being present in the moment.

Unsubscribing from the email list vs. letting your inbox build.

A healthy snack after a workout vs. binging later because you're hungry.

Organization and Preparation

That's it. It's not a secret. Organization and preparation, that's the cheat code. Structure your life to save your strength. If you want to create a simple and efficient label for adjusting your environment to support your willpower and discipline, prepare and organize your life, and you'll see the rewards. Fewer decisions, less temptation, less stress, and fewer mistakes.

"Wow, Nick, this is good stuff. I've never thought of this before."

Sure, you have, Chad, you have, actually! You just don't apply it when and where it matters.

169

- Keeping a phone charger in our car in case our battery gets low.

- Having water on the nightstand in case we get thirsty at night.

- Putting keys on a hook by the front door so we don't lose them.

- Having a spare tire and a jack in case you get a flat.

- Putting the TV remote on the coffee table so you know where it is next time.

You already design your environment all the time. You're not clueless (not all of you), you just haven't applied the same logic to your goals, standards, and systems. So stop acting like this is new. Start acting like it matters.

You can still win in a bad environment. The self-help gurus will tell you that your surroundings are the death of your discipline. When, really, it's just the start of your regression. A bad environment burns more fuel and energy that you could be using to make the tough calls or fight the harder battles. Your environment isn't the only thing that kills your discipline, but it's part of it. And it eats you from the inside out.

And if your environment doesn't drown you, the people around you just might.

- φ Your environment either feeds your focus or bleeds you dry.
- φ You don't rise to your goals; you fall to your setup.
- φ Change your environment and consistency stops being a fight.

Excuses vs. Truths

Excuses	Truths
I can't focus when I work from home.	Stop working next to where you binge TV.
I have a hard time avoiding the sweets in the fridge.	Stop fucking buying them.
I just need more willpower.	You need fewer temptations.
I can handle distractions.	You're handling them straight into stagnation.
It's not that big of a deal.	Every "not big deal" compounds into failure.

Challenge Question

What's one part of your daily environment that's quietly draining your discipline, and what's the simplest change you could make to fix it?

Tighten Your Inner Circle

We all have those people who we know just aren't our allies, no matter what we do. We can be the friendliest individuals, but every time they get the chance, they'll either talk us down, disagree with us, question our motives, or shoot down our ideas. We put up walls against them and their tactics because we know they'd sooner see us gone than succeed.

What if I told you that these people are just roadblocks to maneuver around, that they aren't really part of the problem? That you'll smile at their reaction to your new mindset? That those aren't the people who will be sabotaging you every step of the way?

You'll spend half your life guarding against strangers, only to realize the knife stabbing you was being wielded by someone who swore they loved you.

The ones who are going to derail you and take your eye off the ball, it'll be your friends and family. They'll hand you excuses. They'll soften your standards. Then they'll call it *love.* You'll defend their intentions. You'll tell yourself they mean well. But deep down, you'll feel it, the weight of every 'be careful' and every 'you've changed.' It's death by a thousand comforts.

You won't walk away angry. You'll walk away heavy because you hopefully understand not everyone deserves to come with you.

When Growth Triggers Guilt

Your growth will trigger those who aren't growing. Not because you are doing something wrong, but because you'll be proving to them what they can't or refuse to do.

It's not jealousy at first. It's shame dressed up as irritation. When you start stacking wins, you make people audit their own effort without saying a word. They'll tell themselves you got lucky, that you have more time, that you don't understand their situation. It's easier for them to rewrite your story than face the part of theirs that's stuck.

Whether you mean to or not, you'll become the one holding up a mirror and causing people to see the reflection that they've been avoiding.

Here's the real shift. In their eyes, you stop being their friend and start being their reminder.

You'll notice it in small moments. Their cheers start to sound forced. They no longer ask about your progress, and when they do, it's often accompanied by a quick joke or a sudden topic change. It's not because they stopped caring; it's because your effort reminds them they stopped trying.

When they give you the barrage of questions and "yea, buts" to try to get you off your path, just remember it's not an attack. They'll dress it up as concern. But watch closely, it's guilt talking. Guilt rarely shows up loud. It hides behind sentences that sound polite. 'You're taking this too seriously.' Or 'Don't forget to live a little.' 'I just don't want you to burn out.' They sound caring, but what they really mean is, 'Stop reminding me what discipline looks like.' That's not love talking—that's self-preservation. People prefer the version of you that doesn't challenge them and make them feel little.

The people you spend a lot of time with are a different story, though. You see them often enough that they act like your increasingly shining light makes them look dimmer. And you know what, it can. But that's not your problem; it's theirs. They are the ones who can either shape the fuck up or get out of your way. Blood or not. They don't even know they're doing it. Most of the time, it's instinct, the mind protecting itself from the truth that it could be doing more. Guilt isn't evil; it's just easier than effort. It hurts because these are the people you'd bleed for. But the truth doesn't care who you love.

Spotting Subtle Sabotage

You'll find that the most supportive people in your new journey are going to be the people who are actually in your corner, as well as some of the most random strangers. I remember one morning when I stopped by the gas station to

175

get my morning energy drink, and the kind lady behind the counter asked me how my day was going with a smile on her face. I was having a pretty good morning. My workout felt great, and I had hit a new weight loss milestone.

"Going pretty good actually! I weighed in today at 50 pounds lost!" Not my exact words, but it was something along those lines.

The smile that shot across her face was bright enough to make you think that I just gave her the single greatest piece of news she's ever heard. I don't remember quite what she said afterwards, but I do remember how it made me feel. Her best wishes and excitement for me filled me with delight and empowerment for the rest of the day. I had no connection to this woman; my results from my string of smart habits meant nothing to her character and had no effect on who she was as a person. This stranger had no stake, no guilt, no ego, just joy. That's what support feels like when there's no insecurity to defend.

A coworker later that day tried his best to convince me to pitch in for pizza. Knowing that I was nowhere near done and still in the midst of my 75Hard, failing would mean starting back at day one. He still pushed further.

"You've lost 50 pounds, celebrate it. You've earned it."

At this point, I was accustomed to waving off such persuasion attempts. It's the perfect example of how people expose themselves, the ones who want to see you win, and the ones who don't give a damn if you crash.

Some of these tactics they use are easy to spot. But once you start seeing them, you can't unsee them.

"You're taking this a little too seriously, I think." This sounds like concern, but your commitment is really just making them uncomfortable. They want you to tone it down, so they don't have to level up.

"Don't forget to live a little." What sounds like friendly advice is really, "Please stop reminding me that I'm wasting my potential."

"You're changing...." They feel threatened because they are losing their influence over you. What they really are saying is, "I liked you better when you were easier to control."

However, sometimes those who claim to have your back are better at hiding it. You start doubting, and they talk you back up. You cheer and they cheer right with you, but as we know, actions speak louder than words.

You'll say you want to skip the party because there's alcohol and you want to avoid the temptation. They say they understand and it's a good idea, but they're grumpy about it or stop inviting you in general instead of giving you a choice.

They "believe in you..." but consistently play devil's advocate. "I support it, but I just want you to think it through." Caution is smart, but constant skepticism is sabotage.

They ask about your goals or how the journey is going, but they never hold you accountable to them. The moment you begin to slack, they'll support that. "It's okay, get back on it next week." If they were truly supporting you, they'd try to get your ass back in gear instead.

They'll give you the "Let me know how I can help," bit, but never follow through. If you have to beg for support, you never actually had it.

When Relationships Can't Keep Up

Most of this isn't evil. It's not personal. They just can't grow with you, and it's on you to recognize that before it drags you backward.

I noticed how much smaller my circle became as friendships burned out, became stale, or were cut entirely. And it was an equal mix between me leaving and others walking out. And that's okay.

You aren't heartless for distancing yourself; you're focused. And not everyone is ready to come with you. And if you drag them, you'll waste your time and slow yourself down.

The reality is that people change and they evolve. The gap between you doesn't stay empty; it fills with resentment, guilt, and wasted energy.

You'll see it in the smallest moments first: money, habits, how you spend your time.

That friend who wants to split a DoorDash but is aggravated because you packed a lunch to save money. Now *you* are costing him more money because he has to pay the whole bill himself.

You are being told that you are suddenly disagreeable with everything because you started looking at things with a new, mature mindset. Or that guy who says you don't hang out enough anymore because you don't want to smoke weed every day, and that's all he's into.

Here's a real one. I had a friend who made a joke that I was becoming a corporate bozo because I was taking my career "too seriously." Apparently, learning the lingo, reading about and practicing corporate communication, paying more attention to my verbal filter, and dedicating some of my free time to work projects meant that I was selling out.

He's got a college education; I don't. Over the past four years, I have nearly doubled the annual salary we were earning (and he still is). I have an open sky of career growth ahead of me, while he's looking forward to his next paycheck the day after he gets paid. I'll accept being a bozo, I guess.

Don't Trade Shit for Poop

People will think that you are giving 200% to improve yourself just because they are giving 100%.

They'll assume you're obsessed, overdoing it, or trying to prove something because your pace exposes their comfort.

Remember that our capacities are not equal. It's not that you are giving 200%. It's just that they need to give 100% to achieve the same results as you got with 50%.

179

Just be sure that you are increasingly self-aware of potential new and growing flaws. We'll talk more about toxic self-accountability later. But suppose you are skipping out on responsibilities in pursuit of self-improvement, leaving other people to pick up after you. In that case, you're really just trading shit for poop. You quit drinking but pick up online shopping. You cut out junk food but start binging validation. You hit the gym every day but stop showing up in your own home.

Remember the chapter about excuses? Yeah, don't use your self-improvement as an excuse to skip out on other things.

Stop Carrying People Who Aren't Moving

Cutting certain people will be easy since they won't fight it. A lot of them won't even deserve a confrontation. Sometimes you just need to stop texting back, and they'll do the rest. You'll even find that cutting some people out of your life is more for your sanity instead of growth.

That person who's always negative about every single thing? It makes it hard to stay positive and keep moving forward. *Leave.*

That friend who is always having drama? You start to see that they're the reason behind all of it. *Gone.*

That person who says that *all men/women* are (insert expletive), well, guess what? You'll be one less for them to deal with. *Bye, Felicia.*

180

Keeping the wrong people in your life doesn't make you loyal. It keeps you stuck. Your time and energy are currency. Stop spending them on people who never pay you back. That friend who always bails, that sibling you're always defending, at some point, you have to stop handing out free passes.

If you have to shrink your goals, standards, or values to fit into your circle, you're in a cage. And the emotional toll of always being the "motivated one" will either wear you out or piss you off. You'll either dump the group or you'll crumble back into their comfort zone.

My first experience in this was a newly formed Dungeons & Dragons group (yes, I'm a nerd, and I love it). We'd spend Saturdays laughing, eating junk food, and building worlds our Dungeon Master had worked his ass off to create. For a while, it was one of the highlights of my week.

Over time, though, the energy changed. The group began learning more about each other, but not all of it aligned. Politics crept into the breaks. Little jabs turned into debates. A few of the players leaned harder into social and moral causes. While I respected their efforts, the energy just didn't match mine. We were still laughing, but the connection was starting to feel off.

Towards the end, I was knee-deep in self-improvement, working out, eating clean, and climbing fast at work. Every other Saturday, I'd drive an hour and a half to be the old man at a table full of twenty-somethings, figuring life out. They talked about college stress and weekend plans. I was talking about saving, investing, discipline, and next steps. It hit me one week, is this still good for me? Or am I just holding on to what's fun, but not progressive?

So it was time to make a decision. The group tensions, views, and lifestyles were no longer benefiting me and were holding me back.

The crazy thing is, from why I could tell, I was the only one feeling this way. There was no motion to end the campaign or make any changes. The group dynamics as a whole were functioning just fine, but I found myself drifting away. That was my problem, not theirs. Sometimes the distance isn't a betrayal, it's a boundary. I was surrounded by people I liked, but couldn't grow with at the time.

When Love Stops Growing with You

Sometimes growth kills love, not because anyone did something wrong. One person starts moving, the other stays still. And at first, it's fine, until it isn't. The distance grows quiet, and then heavy. One starts resenting the change, the other resents being held back. That's not drama, that's just circumstance.

Remember that both people in a relationship should be benefiting from one another. You should both be adding value, not trading energy. A relationship isn't 50/50; it's two people giving 100/100. If you're pushing forward and they're pulling you back, that's not partnership, that's resistance. So, if you find yourself trying to grow but your partner keeps purposely pulling you back into your bad habits and mindsets, then you need to seriously consider how useful they are in your life. I don't care if you've been together one year or twenty. You are allowed to grow; they're not allowed to hold you down.

However, things are always a bit more complicated than that. In many scenarios I've read about, it wasn't so much about the partner holding the growing person back; it was just that they didn't want to grow as well.

You'll find that as you adapt and your mindset changes, not only do your standards for yourself change, but those of the people around you as well. The things you begin to value resonate, and you'll want to see those values within the people you spend your time with.

You start changing your habits — eating cleaner, training harder, showing up for yourself every day. You want them to join you, not because you're better, but because you know what better feels like. But they're content. And that's when the distance begins—not from a lack of love, but from a lack of movement.

Unfortunately, your partner is unwilling to start a diet or exercise. They are happy where they are. That might be mildly in shape, or a full-on elephant who's two donuts away from a heart attack.

Are they obligated to jump on your journey as well, just because you are? In my opinion, not at all. It's their job to be supportive, not necessarily involved. Your journey is just that, yours. Not theirs.

However, your wants and needs are also allowed to change. You may find yourself wanting "different." And that's okay. But it's also okay that they don't want to be "different."

You need to be willing to weigh whether them not being on the same journey or mindset is worth rocking the boat. This is only one aspect of the relationship, so does your partner still hold value in other areas of your life? Are you still holding value in theirs?

I'm not a therapist. I'm just telling you, if your growth is creating tension, avoiding the conversation won't save it. Either you both grow through it, or it ends.

The Quiet Between

Sounds lonely, doesn't it? That's because it is. Growth is quiet. It's the long drives with no one texting back. It's eating dinner alone because you stopped saying yes to every distraction. It's scrolling past your old friend group's posts and realizing you no longer belong there. And that's okay. You're not being left out, you're breaking out.

The space that loneliness leaves behind is where better people fit. The quiet between who you were and who you're becoming is meant to test you. It's where you learn to stand on your own before you stand beside someone new.

The old saying that when one door closes, another one opens also applies to people. When you cut your losses, you make room for the individuals in your life who will make a difference. Those losses? That's not failure; it's a reset. Once the dust settles, you'll have room to act like the person you want to be and surround yourself with people of equal values and standards.

- φ The people closest to you can be your biggest anchors.
- φ Growth exposes weak relationships; those who loved your comfort, not your progress.
- φ Not everyone deserves to come with you.

Excuses vs. Truths

Excuses	Truths
They mean well.	Good intentions that feed your weakness need to go. They still keep you average.
I owe them loyalty.	They owe you the respect to own your own journey.
They've always been around.	Longevity isn't loyalty.
They're family.	Being family isn't a free pass to drain you.
I don't want to hurt them.	You're not hurting them, you're healing yourself.

Challenge Question

Who around you is still feeding your excuses, and why are you letting them?

Act Like the Person You Want to Be

If you wait for proof, you'll never act. Proof comes after payment. Act like it in choices that cost you, how you eat, how you show up, how you talk to yourself when no one's watching.

Not when you lose 20 pounds. Not when your get your promotion. Not when you feel "ready." You want it? Start acting like you already have it.

You don't get future-you while acting like present-you.

The results aren't immediate; they are downstream from the identity that you'll choose to adopt. Winners act ready before the rest of the world actually is.

The growing lie is that we don't have to put in the effort until we get in a position to receive the results. That lie is what is keeping you stuck.

"I'll start acting like that once I get there."

You don't become a high performer and then earn the right to act like one. The work comes first always. You start acting like the person you want to be, and then you earn the results that follow.

This chapter isn't about pretending to be something you're not. It's about realigning your behaviors, thought processes, decision-making, and identity. You're not pretending, you're becoming.

Your identity isn't a moment. It's your build. Every time you show up when it would've been easier not to, every promise you keep, every kind word you give, and every hard choice you make—those are the things that define you as a person.

Be Skeptical, Not Cynical

Remember the last chapter? This is where it starts. When you start acting differently, people begin to show their true colors.

Are there bogus "habits," toxic routines, and garbage points of view out there? Abso-fucking-lutely. And it's your job and responsibility to conduct research and not accept everything you read as gospel.

In your pursuit to "act like they act," it's vital to have a healthy dose of skepticism around every turn. Being a devil's advocate to everything doesn't have to make you an asshole; just don't confuse awareness with bitterness.

That influencer girl with the tight figure who's telling you how to lose weight with some off-the-wall method, maybe it works, but if you dig and see she has no formal training, hasn't personally trained anyone, and has never been heavier than your left thigh, you might want to pause a moment.

Same with money. Everyone's got a system, and everyone swears theirs is the only way. Some are extreme, some soft; your job is to learn enough to know which fits your life.

For me, it was Dave Ramsey's Snowball and Every Dollar method that helped clear my debt and stop living paycheck to paycheck. Do I follow every single rule he has? Hell, no. Some of them are far too strict for my financial freedoms that I am trying to uphold. Do I understand that his methods are sound and do work regardless? Yes.

Knowing who you follow matters more than copying what they do. Research, question, decide, and once you do, stop apologizing for it. Their opinion doesn't pay your bills.

"Oh, you're only doing that workout because (insert influencer) is doing that."

"Listen here, lard-ass Linda, it's fucking working, ain't it? While you're grabbing the mobility chair because you can't breathe walking to the candy bars at the front register, I'll continue to find what works for me."

These people can be celebrities, politicians, CEOs, friends, family, bosses, whoever. Once you learn to question who to follow, the next move is simple. Go where they are.

Get in the Room

Sometimes, though, just acting like someone else isn't enough if you only see it on your phone or on TV. You also need to surround yourself with the environment you are trying to emulate. This again goes back to keeping your circle tight. Leaving the trash and bringing in people with the mindsets that you want around.

Surrounding yourself with the people you want to mirror, listening, and learning are the prime ways to reproduce their thoughts, processes, decisions, manners, and habits. You learn fastest through proximity. Watch how they move, how they make decisions, and how they handle pressure. Then copy that rhythm until it becomes yours.

Owning your shit doesn't mean doing it alone. Nobody climbs without an example from someone ahead. Getting around people who live the standards you want will push you higher, faster.

And guess what? When you do that, you are going to be the most amateur one there, and that's okay. When you walk into those rooms, expect to be the least experienced one, and take pride in it. It means you're doing something right to be there in the first place.

Be the dumbest person at the table. Be the slowest runner in the group. Be the rookie on the team, or be the weakest in the gym. Their mindset and habits will rub off. You'll see the standards, you'll hear the tips, and you'll feel the momentum. Get comfortable being uncomfortable.

There's a popular idea in beginner hockey. Skate with people better than you, and you'll get better. It couldn't be truer. The first time I joined a higher-level hockey skate, I spent half the time chasing pucks I couldn't catch. Everyone else moved smoother, faster, cleaner. Every mistake I made echoed across the ice. I hated it. But after a few weeks, I started anticipating plays before they happened. My feet moved quicker, my lungs burned longer, and I realized something: just being in that room raised my floor. My whole pace changed. I wasn't the best, but I was no longer the slowest.

You're not in the room just to copy. You're in there to learn lessons for the next time. The room you're scared to walk into is probably the one built to change you.

Mirror vs Calibrate

At work, don't just hear what high performers say, pay attention to how they say it. Yeah, "corporate talk" makes your skin crawl, but it also might be the language of the rooms you say you want to be in.

"I've been trying to take a more strategic lens with my day-to-day, really focusing on high-impact priorities and positioning myself for visibility with leadership."

Here's the thing, though: you want to be where they are. A high performer, someone who has trust and respect. You can't expect a promotion when you're still talking like you're clocking out of an auto shop. The people ahead of you earned trust by showing they can adapt.

"Man, fuck all that. I ain't changin' for nobody. They either deal with it or get the hell outta my face. My skills should be enough."

Okay, Steven, you're 30 years old; you can learn a few new phrases like "action items" or "stakeholders." If all you bring to the table are your "skills," don't be surprised when that's all your boss keeps you for. No one promotes what's replaceable.

Take a pause right here

You're probably thinking, "Wow, Steven sounds like an idiot." You're a little more mature than THAT, right? For sure, you wouldn't use his words. But I'd bet your line of thinking is damn near identical. Do you think changing your ways or "giving in" to the "institution" will make you somehow "less" or a "sellout?"

If the difference between living comfortably and living stressed was whether or not you decided to act a little more like a leader or sound like someone who's ever read a book on communication, what would you do?

A 2016 MIT study found the same thing. People who trained alongside others who performed just a bit better consistently raised their own effort. You rise faster when you're just a little out of your comfort zone.

You don't need a mentor. You need to sit next to someone who makes you feel like you're slacking just by existing. That's the bar you're aiming for. You want to feel lazy? Just hang out with disciplined people.

The people who intimidate you, the ones who talk fast, ask real questions, and actually seem busy because they are getting things done? Those are the people you want to begin conversing with. Sit next to people who make you uncomfortable. Their standards will drag yours higher.

I was somewhat like Steven in our earlier example. When I transitioned out of the blue-collar industry and found myself in my first white-collar job at nearly 30 years old, I immediately felt out of my element. Nice shoes, no hats, clean cuts, and not a single fart joke. My biggest killer, my filter, or lack thereof. You probably haven't been able to tell, but I occasionally like to spice up my sentences with needless fillers.

I was smart enough to read a room and know who my audience was and what I could or couldn't get away with, but being in my first office space, I had yet to learn just how much what I said carried. It was when my manager had a conversation with me about "my brand" that I really started to understand that the things coming out of my mouth did not match my capabilities and room for growth. I was literally betraying myself without realizing it.

Over the years, I have sat in various organizational meetings, had many conversations with individuals who are far outside my pay scale, and been part of many important projects that were important to our customers. I've listened and practiced the words or phrases passed around. Seen what made eyes light up and have used them for myself with various levels of success.

I didn't "sell out" or "drink the punch." I grew the fuck up. I surrounded myself with the examples of how I needed to be. Am I where I want to be yet? Definitely not. But I'm still learning with each lunch I have with another department head, or each project I get to be involved in. I absorb the lessons that are all around. Things I wouldn't be a part of if I stuck with the same people who have literally nothing better to do than bitch and complain about useless shit all day long.

Those people who let leadership live in their heads rent free with nothing better to do than to cry all day long about how things are instead of being a part of the solution? They're dimming their own worth, while your working on yours.

You're not being fake, you're being strategic. You're not copying, you're calibrating. You are putting yourself in a pressure chamber that makes growth unavoidable.

Stop Protecting Your Old Self

Someone's going to call you out for changing. For "selling out." For "not being yourself." They'll say you're mirroring others, trying to be someone you're not.

And here's the thing, they're right, but for the wrong reasons.

You are changing. On purpose. Because your old self was only built to survive your old life. And that life sucked.

People love throwing around the word "authenticity" like it's some sacred law. But often, what they're really saying is, "Don't grow too far beyond me or I'll feel insecure."

If being "authentic" means staying exactly the same, even when that version of you is rooted in fear, laziness, and low standards, then what you're really being is consistent, not courageous.

Nobody's asking you to lie about who you are. This is about refusing to protect the version of you that keeps getting the same shitty results.

Do you honestly believe the best version of yourself will come from defending your old habits, or does it come from throwing yourself into rooms that force you to evolve?

You're not betraying your identity by adapting. You're betraying your potential by refusing to.

So what does calibrating actually look like?

It looks like realizing that interrupting people in meetings doesn't make you bold, it makes you an asshole.

It looks like watching how leaders talk and noticing they don't waste energy in venting circles. They're asking sharper questions and making faster decisions.

It looks like noticing that people at the next level don't gossip, posture, or argue about dumb shit. They outwork, out-listen, and out-execute.

It looks like dropping the idea that being "real" means blurting out your half-baked thoughts in every conversation.

It looks like being aware of how real pros prep, how they recap, how they lead from the middle, even when no one is watching.

It looks like realizing how small you're still playing, and making the decision to level up anyway.

It's not imitation. It's alignment.

And the faster you stop defending your comfort zone as "who you are," the quicker you'll become the version you keep pretending you're working toward.

So start seeking out rooms that make you feel behind.

It makes you sit up straighter.

And it makes you realize how much further you still have to go.

Because that's how you close the gap between who you are and who you're trying to become.

If you are always the most motivated and disciplined person in the room, you're in the wrong fucking room.

- φ Identity is built through repetition, not just achievement.
- φ "Becoming" beats pretending.
- φ Skepticism keeps you sharp. Cynicism keeps you stuck.

Excuses vs. Truths

Excuses	Truths
I'm not that kind of person yet.	Then start acting like you are. Eventually, you will be.
I don't want to be fake.	Growth isn't fake; it's unfamiliar. Only stagnant people call growth fake.
I don't want to look like a try-hard.	Trying hard is what separates progress from pretending.
That's just not me.	Then evolve, that's the whole point.

Challenge Question

Are your daily choices made by the person you are, or the one who you keep saying you want to be?

PART 4:
STAY IN THE
FIGHT

Consistency Is King (and Boring as Hell)

Everyone says they want results, but almost nobody has the stomach for one of the worst parts about getting them. No, it's not the effort, blood, sweat, and tears. Those are the sexy kind of "I earned it" actions.

It's the fuckin' boredom. The quiet drag of brushing your teeth, clocking in, logging miles, checking boxes. The stuff nobody posts about. Doing the same shit day after day after day.

We love to worship intensity, being the driver behind beating the odds, scoring those promotions, or beating our weight loss goals. You've experienced them, those crash diets, the 60-hour work weeks, motivational sprints, the "RAH RAH RAH, let's fucking go" sort of days. Where do those come from, and why do we associate them with the measuring of results and performance?

Motivation, again. That false sense of energy. You've seen the hype videos before any major sporting event: the training, the workouts, the boxing, the teeth gritting, dripping sweat, and looks of pain and determination. Sculpting the ideal course of action towards winning the big game. They are enough to get anybody fantasizing that that's what our journeys should look like.

What those videos don't show? The boring diet that they eat every single day, down to the same chicken and rice bowl, the same measured-out portions, the same refusal of cake at their cousin's birthday. They don't show the 9 p.m. lift on a random Tuesday when the gym is empty, and nobody is filming. You don't see the alarm clock ringing at 5 a.m. for the hundredth morning in a row, when the athlete rolls out of bed sore, tired, and not in the mood, but does it anyway.

Because that doesn't sell. Nobody's clicking a hype reel of silent oatmeal munching, the rhythmic steps on a treadmill for miles, or the early bedtimes. But that's where the fights are, the monotonous work that nobody wants to sit through.

The hardest days of my 75Hard and LiveHard year? The middle parts. The parts where I had habits locked in, and early motivation had faded. The end was just as far away as the beginning. Stuck in the center, thinking to myself, "Well, now what?"

If you can't handle the boring day, who says you can handle the exciting ones?

The Truth About Boredom

Humans are wired to normalize everything we do. We experience and adapt so that we can survive the trials or tribulations around us. We are less stressed when in an equilibrium, so naturally, that's why we try to get there. Remember what we said about balance?

That big promotion? At first, you're grinning like an idiot, ear to ear, in the same office parking lot with a new title and a bigger paycheck. Six months later, you're still dragging ass to the same meetings, except now you've got two more projects dumped on you. What's changed? Nothing, you're still grinding, but the buzz has worn off. That bigger paycheck? Probably nonexistent because your spending grew to match your means.

Six weeks into your diet, staring at a scale like it owes you money. Not a nudge. It must be broken, or your plan isn't working. However, in reality, your body is adjusting, and you need to make adjustments as well. That boredom or stuck feeling? It's just progress hiding in plain sight.

Happiness spikes fade like caffeine; you return to baseline no matter the dose.

This is called Hedonic Adaptation, and it explores why people have a hard time "staying happy." Also called "the hedonic treadmill," it introduces the concept that people have a base level of happiness that they naturally gravitate back to, regardless of life's ups and downs. This phenomenon has been observed in lottery winners many times, where they eventually return to the same level of happiness as they had before winning. In some circumstances, they return to an even lower level of happiness due to changes in relationships and lifestyles brought about by the temporary influx of money. These winners experienced the joy of the money, but did nothing to sustain that joy. Not saving, investing, fixing, or adapting. It came, they spent, and they were poor again.

Recent studies have found that larger winnings, paired with financial adaptation, equaled sustained satisfaction, where the impacts on happiness and mental health were significantly smaller.

It's the same reason the first bite of ice cream hits harder than the thirtieth; pleasure always normalizes.

But if happiness can't hold, then neither can misery. Pain and stress fade as well. This is why someone going through a divorce can eventually laugh again, or after your leg breaks, if you give it time, you'll be running again. The saying, "Time heals all wounds," holds its own in our internal leveling systems as well.

Often, people mistake this leveling out as a sign that something is wrong, as if boredom equals failure. But in reality, boredom = progress on repeat. It means that you have passed your novelty phase and are actually living in the grind itself. Ready for the next push.

Consistency > Intensity

Intensity feels sexy because it's dramatic. It's that "going all in" mindset that people strive to hit. The juice cleanses, the long hours on a work project, the two-a-day workouts. But your body, brain, and life don't build new habits from this; they respond to steady repetition.

Here's a simplistic visual. You start working out and choose the dumbbell bench press as one of your exercises for the day. You grab some 35s, pick your bench, and then struggle through your sets. A day or two later, your muscles hurt, and they're saying, "man, fuck this guy, that sucked. At least it's over."

What happens if you never go back to the gym or do those exercises to work those muscles again? Not much, you just made them hurt for a few days. But now let's add consistency. You start grabbing those dumbbells every Wednesday and hit those bench presses. After a pattern forms, your muscles begin to realize this isn't a phase.

"Holy shit, again with this? Ok, we need to do something about it."

Now you'll start to see your body react. Your muscles begin to grow and become more responsive to your needs. They adapt. They know that because this is becoming a regular thing, they need to be better prepared for it.

Let's say you're at work and have a presentation you need to give. You're not a speech person, and you're putting yourself out there for criticism. Your brain goes into panic mode. Sweating, stuttering, heart pounding, questioning. You survive it, but your brain says, "good thing that shit's over."

If you never do it again, you just stay that same person who's terrified of speaking. But if every week, you're pitching meetings, speaking up in group conversations, or putting yourself out there, your brain is going to realize, "damn, this keeps happening. I'd better build some wiring (confidence) for this."

Over time, the nervousness fades, speeches get smoother, and your outward appearance is reshaped.

I actually experienced this firsthand with this book. A lot of topics that we've covered are in my head, and their arguments are strong and sound. I know what I'm saying, I know how I feel, and where my stances are strong. But if you were to ask me about a particular subject, or the whole book entirely, my answer would be short and sound uneducated.

"I wrote this because myself and everyone on this planet is stupid."

I struggled to get what was in my head, out of my mouth, in the right way.

So I found a way to consistently work on my material, cement my thoughts, and practice speaking out loud.

Every day on my drive to work, I would prompt ChatGPT to pretend to be a podcaster and ask me a series of questions. I would read these out loud and formulate my responses on the spot, just like I would if I were on a podcast. At first, it felt awkward as hell, stumbling, repeating, over-thinking. But soon, I hit a rhythm.

I'd come up with something that sounded good or start getting into a flow with my words. I'd even start commenting on things happening around me during my drive as a catalyst for discussion on self-responsibility. It also made it easier to answer the question "What is your book about?" While my responses aren't necessarily rehearsed, they're practiced. They feel smoother and I've had more time to think about them since I've run through the motions.

The unintended benefits were seen at work. I find myself more comfortable and confident when speaking and presenting in the workplace. There's more trust in myself to deliver the thoughts from my head to my mouth in a clean, organized, and articulate manner.

All from a boring-ass morning commute where I started talking to myself instead of belting out KPop Demon Hunters. "Golden" gets me every time.

This is the boring reality of consistency. Nobody's cheering. Nobody cares. It doesn't feel heroic or intense, but it stacks. And stacked boring reps beat flashy intensity every single time.

The Boredom Filter

We've all hit a "wall" of some sort. That point at which we stop and have to decide whether or not to turn around. That moment in time, you think to yourself, "This was fun, but nah."

The truth is, hitting that wall isn't a sign you're done. And you know it. Every book, movie, video game, and story has those moments of "nowhere to go," but the protagonist pushes through anyway. That test is something you and I will see all of our lives. But talent, or lack thereof, isn't the answer to break through the wall. It's grit. Angela Duckworth's "grit" research delves into how the best performers aren't always the most talented but rather the most persistent over a longer period of time.

Take Josh Allen, for example. You might know him as the Buffalo Bills' all-star quarterback, but rewind time a little bit, and his story is nothing like a golden-boy prospect. In high school, he wasn't breaking records or making headlines in the newspapers. He was just an average quarterback. No top schools were reaching out, and no one was returning his phone calls. He was never "discovered." He hunted down his opportunities by emailing hundreds of coaches for days and weeks on end until finally landing in JUCO, before moving on to Wyoming. Still not Ohio State, Alabama, or USC. The scouts tore him apart. Poor accuracy and mechanics all over the place. He was "an athlete, not a quarterback."

Most guys stop there. That's their "wall." They accept "not good enough" as the story. But Allen kept with the boring. He kept showing up, kept refining, kept practicing. Every mechanic, every rep, every tape. This turned into progress. One season at a time.

That's grit in action. Those who refuse to quit because things slow down and get boring, dull, or humiliating? They are the ones who find success over those who just have some natural talent. Josh Allen is proof. He didn't stroll into the NFL as a polished prodigy. He worked through years of obscurity, rejection, and unglamorous games until consistency rewired him into one of the most dangerous quarterbacks in the league.

Talent got him a tryout. Grit got him a career.

If You Can't Handle Boring, You'll Never Handle Winning

So, where does this tie in to so many of our lives? Everywhere!

Your financial freedom is most likely not going to come from a big, unexpected bonus or lottery win. It'll be carved into the budgeting foundation you stick to every single day. Skipping stupid purchases, saving instead of spending, living minimally instead of lavishly. That 401(k) is built paycheck by paycheck. Not in a single deposit.

Your health won't come from a weekend 5K or a couple of months in the gym. It'll be from those daily walks to keep your joints loose. It'll come from skipping the damn muffins and eating a freaking apple instead. It'll be from keeping those "useless" doctor check-ups on the calendar, even though you are feeling fine. Longevity is built on choices so dull that nobody claps for them.

Relationships? Same thing. They aren't your honeymoon or family vacations. They are the daily check-ins, the dishes after work, and the listening when you're tired. The showing up to your friend's event because they'd love to see you there. Your family, friends, and loved ones need your boring days to be as reliable as your fun ones.

Promotions won't come because you can do a project once. They happen because you are trusted. Your reliability is proven from the grind you put in every single day. It's being able to handle the menial shit so consistently that when big things show up, they don't have to question whether you'll deliver. Reliability is forged in the boring grind. That's the trait that makes people bet on you when it counts.

Self-responsibility is realizing that winning isn't some big highlight reel. It's a mountain of a thousand boring pebbles.

Winning is boring, but it's just done longer, harder, and better than everyone else who is willing to quit.

- φ   The hardest part of success isn't effort, it's boredom.
- φ   Grit outlasts talent because boredom kills drive.
- φ   Results come from small, dull, daily commitments.

Excuses vs. Truths

Excuses	Truths
It's too repetitive.	Good, then it should be easier to keep going.
I've been doing it for weeks without any changes.	Either make an adjustment, or keep going.
I'll take a day off and get back on track.	Momentum dies quietly while you rest loudly.
It's too hard to keep up.	Hard is the toll to ride success.
I'll do it later.	Later is the oldest lie you tell yourself.
I've earned a break.	You've earned better habits, not holidays.

Challenge Question

If no one ever clapped again, would you still show up tomorrow?

Stay Humble, Stay Dangerous

Are you the guy who parks his dually in the Low Emissions parking spot or the employee who parks in the visitor spots, all so you don't need to walk your mouth-breathing ass farther to the building? Do you have a nice car and refuse to use a single spot? Always at a 45-degree angle and taking up two handicap spots at once? I'm looking at you, Cadillac guy, at every local supermarket.

Are you that lady who just can't be wrong, no matter what evidence is thrown in front of you? You somehow just know everything about anything? Maybe you have a habit of "one-upping" everybody? They share an achievement, and your way to converse is to share your "relatable" but better achievement.

Or are you that person who, instead of being teachable, hides behind your title, years of experience, age, or the money you've spent? "I'm 55 years old, I...."

When your boss has approached or emailed you about something you've done, have you ever thought to yourself or told someone else that you're being "targeted" or "yelled at?" Even though nothing about the situation was ever accusatory?

None of those are you, right? Surely you're a bit more evolved and mature than that? We've all experienced those kinds of people. Stuck in their ways, shrouded and hiding behind ego. The people who give their parents, bosses, or coworkers shit every chance they get, while at the same time they act like the biggest children.

And if they're corrected, you might as well have kicked their dog. God forbid someone could be in the wrong or receive negative feedback without taking it as a direct assault on their character and life.

This type of behavior and ego-driven actions are nothing short of pride. Your ill-placed pride and the way you *think* others see you mask how people actually see you. It keeps you stuck. Even if you read this book 10 times over, if you let your pride get in the way of your growth, you'll lose the game. Every time. Your ability to control your ego and accept humility will lift the veil between you and the rest of your life. As long as you understand that ego is weakness and humility is strength.

Humility Is a Weapon, Not a Weakness

Humility is what keeps your pride and ego in check. Are you allowed to be proud of yourself, the things you have, and what you can accomplish? Fuck, yeah! Are you allowed to let that get in the way of further accomplishments or move you forward at the expense of others? Fuck, no!

Humility and humbleness aren't soft. In fact, at first, it's much harder to recognize and accept being in the wrong, being the smaller person, or needing an attitude adjustment. The most dangerous person in the room isn't always the loudest; it's the one who is absorbing, adapting, and learning.

That's the guy who is eventually outpacing.

You got to where you are today by learning. Your relationship, your finances, your work, your choice of friends, your attitude. All of it was learned values and behaviors. Which means you can continue to learn, grow, and adapt these things. But you need to be able to accept that part of learning and growing is fucking up, being wrong, and being okay with it—using wrong moves, choices, and mistakes as a lesson to better yourself for next time.

But you won't be able to get there if you keep using your ego as a shield to protect your fragility. If humility is the accelerator, then ego is the brake.

Now hold up a big mirror here and stare directly into yourself and find these ego-isms that you probably fall victim to. On first pass, you are probably going to think that you don't fall into any of these, but chances are, your own ego is protecting itself from being called out.

The Fragile Feedback Victim

If your boss calls, pulls you aside, or sends you an email regarding a task or situation that may not have been handled correctly, and you may have had a hand in it, what's your first reaction? Do you immediately get defensive? Probably, it's only natural to want to save face. But how do you do it? Do you assume that you're being targeted? Do you think you are being yelled at, even though the email is professionally written? Do you twist their words into something they aren't? What if someone tells you that's not the intent of the message? Are you still taking offense? Are you keeping yourself as the victim, or are you immediately looking for something to finger-point at? Maybe it's not all your fault, but are you looking for somewhere you could have improved upon?

Maybe you got pulled over, and your first instinct is to meet the officer with a combative attitude instead of hearing out why you were stopped in the first place.

Your significant other approaches you with an issue they are having about your relationship. Do you defend yourself by finding a flaw of theirs? Just because you messed up doesn't mean you need to meet it with opposition.

Receiving feedback is one of the most important aspects of growth and self-accountability. While you can self-audit, there will always be things that you're blind to. Feedback is free ammo; dangerous people beg for it.

Reply with "Thanks for flagging. Here's what I'll change by Friday." Then do it.

Short, adult, lethal.

The Unteachable Veteran

You've been where you're at, doing what you're doing, seeing what you've seen for so long, that you have this false sense of experience. You couldn't possibly learn anything new. You've muddied up the differences between tenure and mastery.

Your children are buying a new car, and maybe they are telling you about the financing route they're exploring. It's a method you're unfamiliar with. It's not how you've always done it, and you're unsure of the pros and cons. Of course, you want to help, but instead of hearing them out and learning with them, you don't want to risk sounding uninformed. So you tell them, "That's not how you do it. Do it like this." Instead of learning and helping, you are now just preaching and annoying. Chances are, you've done things like this so often that you don't even notice people don't ask for advice from you unless they have to.

You've been in your current role for over two decades and have held numerous positions in various departments. While you use your experiences in those departments to shape your decisions, you don't take the time to realize that it's been over a decade or longer since your time spent in that role. Things change all the time, and you just sound like an uninformed know-it-all. If your current role still involves how another department operates, but you aren't taking the time to keep up with the times, you're going to be left behind in the dust by those who grow in the role and are up to date with current procedures and processes. Humility keeps you leveling up.

Maybe you're that veteran at work who finds the small tasks menial. You won't outright say that they're beneath you, but you leave them for everyone else to do. When in reality you actually just don't know how to do them, and you just won't admit to it.

Say, "Teach me how you're doing it now." Take notes. Pick one thing to adopt this week.

Keeps dignity, establishes growth.

The Story-Topper

When someone is telling you a story, are you listening and coming up with questions? Are you interacting and keeping THEIR narrative going? Or are you consistently hearing what they say and relating it to something in your life? Are you making THEIR story about YOU? As they're speaking, are you just waiting for your turn to respond?

Your friend is telling you about an incredible accomplishment they had, and it's somewhat similar to one of yours. Are you just waiting to tell them about YOUR thing? It's similar but better. They got a silver ribbon in archery over the weekend. That's cool, and you know it is, but for some reason, you have the urge to tell them about how years ago you got a gold ribbon in the 100m dash. Remember how I said earlier that on the path of self-accountability, you will find people who don't want or care about you succeeding? That your growth will put a spotlight on their lack of growth, and that these are the people holding you back? Well, without meaning to, you've become that person in their life they should be leaving behind. Humility listens, ego performs.

Ask your friend two follow-up questions before sharing anything about yourself. Make their story bigger, not yours.

Simple ratio forces humility.

The Person Who Can't Be Wrong

You know this person. Doesn't matter what the topic is, sports, politics, or your line of work. They act like they've got a master's degree in all of it. You could spend ten years building expertise in your field, but the second you mention it, they're right there nodding like they're your equal, if not your superior. And the moment you present something that doesn't match their opinion, they're either digging in for an argument or twisting their words mid-conversation to make it sound like they were "actually" saying the same thing you just corrected them on.

Here's the truth: they aren't learning. They're performing. They're protecting ego, not building competence. And when ego is the driver, you stall. If you're the person who refuses to say "I don't know," then you've just put a ceiling on your own growth. You've made ignorance permanent.

Think about it, when was the last time you heard someone like this ask a real question? Not a fake setup to argue, but an actual question meant to understand? You haven't, because in their world, asking is seen as a weakness. The irony is that the truly dangerous people, the ones who rise faster and adapt

219

quicker, are the ones who ask the most questions. They're humble enough to admit they don't have the whole picture, and that humility turns into an advantage.

If this is you, fix it. Stop defending, stop shifting goalposts, stop hiding behind smug nods and "Well, that's what I was saying." Try shutting your mouth and asking one question in every conversation you have this week. Because the day you stop needing to be right is the day you actually start getting better. Humility sharpens, ego dulls.

Say, "I might be wrong." Ask one clarifying question before you argue.

Negative Feedback as Growth Fuel

Do you think you could sit down with your partner, friend, parent, or boss and ask them, "Where am I fucking up? Where can I do better?" Do you think you could actually mean it and not take offense or react defensively? Not make excuses or become combative?

Why are we so afraid of feedback, and why do we react so negatively towards it when it isn't in our favor? Why do we take it as such an attack on our character?

It should be so simple and easy, right? We take positive feedback naturally. "Hey, you, keep doing it like that, it's working." Okay, so you keep the course. But the moment you hear, "No, not that way, it's not working." Flags fly, walls rise, and guns come out. Why?

It's partly because we all have this image of ourselves in our heads. How we assume the world perceives us. What we want to be known for, seen as, capable of. Our identity is closely tied to our self-esteem, especially our strengths. And when something comes around that challenges it, we see holes in our own armor that we've been ignoring, maybe on purpose.

Another part depends on who is giving us the feedback. You'll see this more in the workplace. Let's say you really don't like your manager. Enough so that when you're working, their presence ruins your whole mood. You get to your one-on-one meeting, and he mentions that he has noticed a dip in your performance. You don't like the guy, and his giving you this negativity, whether you realize it or not, makes you feel smaller than him. So, you lash out; you need control back. You don't want this guy to feel superior to you.

You need to grow up. Because you've now taken offense and become aggressive, you've further soured the relationship you have with him, and it'll affect more than just the two of you. Chances are, you aren't the only one acting like a child. He's got seven more children he needs to round up, all of them giving him shit for one reason or another. Eventually, he will react less individually and more collectively towards the group. Now everyone is going to suffer from some rule or policy change.

"But Niiiiiiiiick, if he were a better manager, he would…."

Shut the fuck up.

221

If you are still thinking this way, you will need to reread this book. By now, you should have started to realize that, regardless of external circumstances, you are in control of your actions and reactions.

Yes, negative feedback doesn't feel good, especially when it comes as a surprise.

"But Niiiiiiiiiiiick, I wouldn't mind the negative feedback if it was balanced with some positive...."

You are 24, 28, 35, or 50 years old. If you NEED to be made to feel good before someone tells you something negative, I'm sorry, but you need to figure that the fuck out. Where's your own self-worth?

Should a leader be able to see your strengths as well as your weaknesses? Very much so. But you shouldn't have to hear that just to be "validated."

Once you realize that negative feedback is a tool to be used, your world opens up. When you can be told what you're bad at, without drama, you become that friend who can be counted on. That partner who can grow with the relationship. That employee who can be trusted to correct an error.

Negative feedback is such a powerful tool that you should be seeking it out. Your relationship with your partner can go from good to great if you know what's in the way. At work, for all you know, there could be a promotion sitting on the other side of simply getting rid of the neck beard that makes you look homeless.

At my current company, I participated in a side project that involved completing a Korn Ferry 360 Assessment. Simply put, it was a high-level personality test designed to help me identify my strengths and weaknesses. I completed it myself and had to ask several coworkers and peers to complete it as well. For them, it was basically a "How do you believe Nick handles himself in these situations as both a peer and a leader, and how do you think he could improve upon them?"

At around just over 100 questions, it was comprehensive. It was completely anonymous, and out of the nearly 30 people I tried to convince to take this, I received 11 results. These 11 people helped reshape many aspects of how I carried myself and how I acted as a teammate.

The most valuable comments that came from the whole thing were the negative ones. The ones that I could work on to improve how I was perceived within the office. Here are a few that made the most impact.

"Can tell the knowledge is there and the personal drive to make the right decision is there. Just think G that speed sometimes comes into play and causes some missed decisions. Recommend just slowing down and making sure everything is correct before moving onto the next task." To this day, I still have to remind myself of this. To slow down and not work at 90 mph.

"Needs to conduct themselves with professionalism." Blunt and to the point. Fixed.

"May need to work on professionalism a bit in some meetings/team settings, but overall very easy to talk to and build a working relationship with." Another reminder of how my loose language was affecting someone, and I had no idea.

"...I just have a little issue with the execution. Sometimes can come off a little hostile/rough on trainees at times." This was particularly surprising because I had always seen training as one of my favorite strengths. To hear that I came off harsh was not something I expected in *this* area. A few years later, here I am writing a book and trying to teach people to stop being dickheads.

This was a huge undertaking, and it really took putting my big boy pants on to sit here and not scoff at any remark that was made against me. But with it, I truly learned the value of hearing where I was going wrong and the things that I couldn't see for myself. Even to this day, during my occasional check-ins with my manager, I continue to look for areas for improvement. Every failed task, every misplaced word, and every stray comment were weapons to push further and continue my growth.

Fragile people crumble, dangerous people sharpen.

The Toxic Side of Radical Responsibility

Of course, with all good things, it must be in moderation. You'll get into this rhythm when you start seeing the bullshit and excuses in other people around every corner.

"Look at this dude, speeding in a parking lot."

"That mindset is shit, if they thought like an adult."

Seeing these things shows that you are now starting to recognize poor self-responsibility in others, and hopefully catching it in yourself as well. But that doesn't give you a free pass to start thinking that you are better than every other person in the room. You've got to remember that while you're on the growth path, you can't force it on others who aren't there yet. Yes, is their laziness annoying? Sure, but you still need to be in control of your shit and can't be treating others as such.

Don't become a self-righteous asshole, and be careful not to fall into the "I've been well behaved, so I deserve..." trap. Your newfound discipline shines a light on you, but it doesn't give you a license to look down on others just because you can.

Humility will make you dangerous. It will keep you learning, listening, and improving while others defend, deflect, and decay.

While the next chapter dives deeper into how our self-accountability doesn't just help you, it helps others, don't forget to check your ego in the mirror. If you don't, you'll just end up being the Cadillac guy at the supermarket.

- φ Ego is weakness dressed as confidence.
- φ Humility is the skill that keeps growth alive.
- φ Pride stops progress by making feedback feel like an insult.

Excuses vs. Truths

Excuses	Truths
I already know that.	Then why aren't you better at it?
They're just targeting me.	Are they? Or are you being sensitive?
I don't need advice.	Everyone does, especially the proud.
I've been doing this long enough.	Time served doesn't mean mastery earned.
I don't make mistakes.	Thinking that is your biggest one.

Challenge Question

When was the last time you received negative feedback and weren't insulted by it?

Quit Wrecking Our Shit with Your Shit

Alright, you've made it this far, so you may as well stick around for arguably the most important chapter, "Quit Wrecking Our Shit With Your Shit." Simply put, stop being a taint on the rest of society.

When you can't control yourself, you poison everyone around you. Your piss-poor attitude, your toddler-level impulse control, and your dangerous actions can range from making people sigh whenever you enter the room to putting people's lives in danger.

It's time to realize that the world doesn't revolve around you. Yes, it's up to you to fix your life, but your life affects everyone else.

Own Your Sh*t: You're the Problem

This isn't about charity, heroism, or sainthood. I'm not encouraging people to go out into the world looking for every opportunity to be Mother Teresa. I'm looking for neutrality at a minimum. Stop being the human equivalent of secondhand smoke: unwanted, toxic, and choking the rest of us out.

The Cadillac guy who takes up two handicap parking spots, littered with entitlement. "I own this nice car, so I'm obliged to protect it. It's okay that someone has to park somewhere else." Well, now another handicapped person, maybe worse off than you, has to park at the end of the lot.

"The trash compactor needs to be run, even though it's a simple push of a button, I'll just drop this trash bag here, it's not my problem." Now you're starting a chain of other assholes doing the same, and soon the whole compactor area is looking and smelling like a disgusting garbage dump. Simply because you refused to hit the button.

You walk into the office at 8 a.m., but until you've had your morning coffee and wake up a little bit, you're an absolute cunt. I'll tell you right now, Tammy, no one thinks it's cute that you're "not a morning person." You're a grown-ass adult who's acting like a cranky toddler. Your coworkers groan when you show up.

Perhaps you're the coworker who always has something to complain about. Doesn't matter what kind of day it is, you throw those jokes around like, "Oh man, I could just yeet myself out that window right about now." Goofy occasionally, but when you're saying it every day and multiple times at that, you're killing the mood. Some people are there to make a living and don't need you downing the place. If you don't like it that much, shut the hell up and quit. Guarantee that most of your coworkers will be happy about it. Or better yet, start trying to be a part of the solution instead.

Most parking lots have a speed limit of about 15 mph unless otherwise posted. Do you go over that? Do you go 15 mph because that's what you're "allowed" to do? Or do you drive at a safer and slower speed to protect those around you? You're the one driving a multi-ton vehicle. Do you take ownership that even though people should be looking where they are walking, it's YOUR responsibility to not run someone over?

Are you the kid who is constantly causing trouble and distress within the family? They give, give, give, and yet you make everything a problem. You make every excuse you can, and it's never your fault. False promises, never owning your mistakes, and always thinking about the greener grass on the other side. But in reality, you're the one who's killing the grass with every action and decision you make out of convenience or laziness.

Neutrality vs. Moral Math

How often have you heard someone try to justify their negative behavior by trying to pad or save it with some kind of righteous act? It's pretty easy to spot these kinds of things because the audacity is awe-inspiring. Yet, even though it's such obvious garbage, we still hear it.

"It's fine that I screamed at my wife last night, I'll buy her flowers on the way home from work."

"I might be a little hungover at work today, but that's okay because I've been killing it this month."

"It's okay that I didn't pick up that trash I dropped; I helped clean a park last weekend."

Pretty blatant crap, isn't it? Things like this scream, "I don't care about the places or people around me." Convenience outweighs courtesy by a heavy margin. But what if you narrowed the scope a bit to more interpersonal things that may not be readily apparent?

"I ignored my family all week, but I posted a nice family photo on Facebook."

"I've shown up late a few times recently, but I'll stay a few minutes late today to show I'm committed."

"I ghosted my buddy's text, but I liked his Instagram post, so I still count as a good friend."

We're all guilty of this kind of Moral Math-ing, it's just another way of Negotiating With Ourselves. But instead of these internal battles affecting our growth, they're now affecting those around us. But neutrality here isn't about doing a good deed just to allow a bad one. It's about starting from 0. At a minimum, we shouldn't be going about our lives in a way that shits on other people.

Neutral is throwing your trash away. Negative is throwing it on the ground. Positive is picking up someone else's trash. You're taught this your whole life while growing up. However, for some reason, people often forget this as they "figure life out." People think they are a good person because they didn't murder someone today, but they sped through the Kroger parking lot and got lucky that no one stepped in front of their car.

It's simple behavior adjustments that a child can understand. Neutrality is simply about not being a fucking problem. But as we grow older and learn more about the world, we start finding it easier to team up with each other to blame other groups or systems, simply to excuse our own behaviors.

Good deeds don't erase harm; they only add to zero *after* you stop the harm.

Ground-Level Rot

The whole core of this book. Calling out the way people love to point fingers at the government, politicians, billionaires, corporations, or some controlling power for their frustrations with the people around them. Here's another reality check: Washington isn't creating a piss-poor culture; it's Chad in the seat next to you who chews like a cow and leaves crumbs all over his desk. It's not your government's fault that your local grocer is closing down; it's that they have been broken into three times and need to raise prices to cover the losses. It's that everyone keeps shopping at Amazon and Walmart instead of supporting small businesses.

People want to complain about car insurance rates while there are people driving like idiots getting into wrecks and causing the rates to jack up. Or complain about lying politicians, but go around and lie to their spouse, friends, boss, and kids daily.

Culture collapses from the ground up. Sure, pressure can be applied from above, but when people stop showing respect to one another, and we begin to alienate ourselves, we lose accountability and start taking advantage of each other.

But macro culture examples can go down 10 different rabbit holes. It's easier to think about smaller examples.

When you were growing up and either Mom or Dad was in a pissy mood, how often did it affect the whole household? Everyone was probably walking on eggshells. And if someone got caught in the crossfire, their mood was ruined, and it only got worse from there.

Or your friend group, when one friend needlessly goes off the rails, think about how it stirs the whole pot. Sides get taken, arguments start. Now, everyone is stressed and being affected just because of that one person. The best-case scenario is that they work it out; the worst-case scenario is that it causes a divide, and now the group is no more.

In traffic, it only takes one entitled shithead to entirely ruin everyone else's commute. Whether they were speeding and lost control, distracted by their phone, or engaging in idiotic road rage, now the highway is shut down and people are stuck. Stepping this up a notch, now that shithead who was weaving in and out of traffic has rescue crews coming out to save their life. Critical resources are being used to save their life. If the timing is poor, those critical resources may not be able to reach another person in time who was just a victim of an untimely accident that wasn't their fault.

This ground-level stuff is what breaks our trust in each other just as much, if not more than, top-down politics. If you are being 100% honest with yourself, I'm absolutely positive that your day, week, or just your mood gets ruined or tainted by random people more often than any President or system.

Nobody Is Bothered; Who Cares?

How often have you done a simple task differently just because you know someone is or could be watching? Like walking all the way to a trash can to throw your trash away, or picking up your dog's poop instead of just leaving it there? Yes, these kinds of things are required by most places because, in some shape or form, you are on somebody else's property. But what about those vague instances when you are in an "eh" kind of place? Where acting a certain way isn't so much required as it is expected. No real consequence one way or another, and there's no one to tell you otherwise. What do you do?

Say you are out in the wilderness and your dog decides the edge of the trail is the perfect place to take his third shit of the day. Yes, there's an expectation to clean it up, but you won't be kicked out and sent packing if you leave it. Nobody is around, so who does it hurt?

Now I'm sure some of you read that and were thinking, "Duh, you should pick it up anyway. What if someone walks by and accidentally steps in it? It stinks, ruins the mood, and is unsightly." I also bet a good portion of people would think, "It's just poop. It's natural and part of the wilderness." Both instances have their validity. If there are no rules or consequences in the made-up place, which argument is correct? Both? Neither? We'll swing back to this in a bit.

This is called a Litmus Test—a situation in which how you act, or what you do when presented with a scenario that has no real rule or consequence to push you one way or another. Sometimes there is an expectation, sometimes not. Simply put, they explain whether someone acts out of self-interest or consideration.

One of the more famous ones is the Shopping Cart Litmus Test, and you've probably heard it before. When you're done unloading your groceries, what do you do with the cart? Do you walk it back to the corral like a civilized person, or do you leave it sitting cockeyed in the middle of the parking lot like a landmine for the next poor bastard trying to park?

Nobody's going to arrest you for abandoning your cart. Nobody's going to fine you or kick you out of the store. If you're quick enough, you don't even have to deal with the judgmental stares. There's zero real consequences.

It's a simple, low-effort responsibility that has no rule forcing you, just an expectation. Returning it takes all of 30 seconds, and yet some people act like it's asking them to donate a kidney. Leaving it says, "My convenience matters more than everyone else's headache." Returning it says, "I'm not a dick, I'll do the bare minimum." You'll hear different excuses as to why they are right, but I have yet to hear one that can't be countered.

Here's the kicker: most people will swear they're "good people." But this test strips that away. Because when there's no law, no cop, no manager breathing down your neck, who are you, really? Are you the kind of person who takes two extra steps to not screw over strangers, or the kind of person who shrugs and drives away because it's "someone else's job?"

The cart doesn't care. The lot attendant probably cares, but society as a whole might not even notice. But that's the point, the Shopping Cart Test isn't about getting caught, it's about proving to yourself whether you can manage the smallest responsibility without being forced.

Returning to the poop scenario, there is no consequence for leaving it, and no reward for picking it up. What are you going to do?

Stack' Em or Scatter' Em

While researching for this chapter, I posted a video on Clapper, the TikTok adjacent platform, asking my own Litmus kind of question: "When you eat at a restaurant, do you stack your plates to make it easier for the Server, or do you leave them as is?" When you go to a restaurant, nowhere do you see that you're required to do this. The expectation is that the server will reach across the table, grab your plates and garbage, and move on. You don't get money off the bill for doing it, but you also don't get charged for not doing it. It costs you absolutely nothing to do this kind gesture, plus it also cleans up your area, giving you more room. Meaning that personal reasons dictate which way you go.

Pretty simple, right? While I was expecting some back-and-forth, I was quite surprised by the responses. With over 90K views and 300 comments, the majority of them, probably over 95%, suggested that most people stack them for the server! Many people say that they stack them, clean up the table, and even push them to the edge to make the server's life easier.

I found a few key things interesting about this. This data suggests that if you go out to eat, you'll see that nearly all people are cleaning up after themselves, but we know that's not the case at all. Bringing up two questions, how many of those 90K views are people who don't clean up, but don't want to out themselves in a comment section heavily leaning one way? And of those individuals, are they not wanting to out themselves because they feel called out for something that they don't do on purpose?

There were a few people who said the expected, "They get paid to do it." But there were quite a few more that were of the mindset that servers have a system for stacking, and when we do it, we screw them up, and they don't like it. As you can imagine, a large number of people commenting were past servers. They were happy to comment that they treat other servers with the same kindness and respect. So, if a significant portion of past servers are helping current servers, it leads me to believe that the "servers don't like it" argument is a myth. Backed up with the fact that not a single server commented against people stacking.

So what does this mean for the people who use the "servers don't like it argument?" Well, maybe misinformation has something to do with it, or they heard it from one or two other servers, or they heard it once and now use it as an excuse to not do it, and feel justified.

Regardless, it highlights how our own attitude and actions can affect those around us, even in simple situations where there are no consequences one way or the other.

And that's the point, not just about stacking plates, but kindness. It's the easiest, cheapest, and most available resource we've got, and somehow the one we ration like it's gold. Kindness costs you nothing. Zero. Not a cent, not a calorie. And yet most people act like it's going to drain their soul to give a little damn about the people around them.

You don't have to write checks or start foundations to make an impact. Sometimes it's as small as giving a nod to the guy who held the door. Those micro moments are what rebuild the foundation of basic decency that's rotting underneath all our self-centered bullshit. They don't make you a saint; they just prove you're not part of the problem.

Kindness isn't weakness, and it's not for optics. It's self-control. You can be tough, direct, and unfiltered while still being kind. The strongest people are usually the calmest ones in the room, because they've learned that snapping, mocking, or bulldozing isn't strength; it's immaturity dressed up in ego.

Something I've learned is that when you start leading with kindness, people remember it. The world's already heavy enough; you don't have to add to it. Your tone, your patience, your small gestures, they ripple. They make it easier for others to breathe, to think, and to show up at their best. It's not about getting credit; it's about not being a fucking burden.

Stop Being The Problem

At the end of the day, this isn't complicated. Neutrality isn't about being a hero, a saint, or a martyr. It's about not being the asshole who makes life harder for everyone else. It's about controlling your moods, habits, and impulses, so you don't pollute the air for the people around you.

Every time you shrug and say, "Not my problem," you may be part of the problem. Every time you justify a shitty act with some half-assed positive one, you're still just doing moral math instead of owning your mess. Society doesn't collapse because of one big event; it erodes because of millions of little daily choices by people who refuse to take responsibility.

The truth is, owning your shit doesn't just change your own life. It keeps you from wrecking everyone else's. And if enough people did that, maybe we wouldn't be drowning in excuses, blame, and finger-pointing. Maybe we'd actually build something worth handing down.

So that's it. Stop being the reason the people sigh when you cross their path. Quit wrecking our shit with your shit.

- ϕ Your lack of discipline bleeds into everyone else's life.
- ϕ Every "not my problem" compounds into a collective decay.
- ϕ Owning your shit makes life easier for everyone, not just you.

Excuses vs. Truths

Excuses	Truths
It's not my job.	That doesn't mean you can't help the situation along.
It's not that big of a deal.	To someone else it might be, though.
It's not my problem.	It becomes everyone's when you ignore it.
Someone else will handle it.	That's the anthem of the irresponsible.
That's just how I am.	Then fix how you are.

Challenge Question

What part of your chaos are you still pretending is harmless to others?

Outro

Alright, here's the deal.

This isn't the part where I pat you on the back or thank you for reading. You don't get a participation trophy for finishing a book about accountability. You made it here because something in you knew it was time to stop bullshitting yourself.

You don't need another quote or a pep talk. You need to take a breath, look in the mirror, and admit what you already know, the only thing standing between where you are and where you want to be is you.

You've been living behind a wall of comfort. You call it "balance," "self-care," or "doing your best," but half the time it's just laziness dressed up nice. You want peace, but you keep feeding chaos. You want success, but you keep negotiating with your own excuses. You've been playing tug-of-war with the mirror and losing.

The hardest truth in this whole book is also the simplest: no one's coming. Not your boss. Not your parents. Not your partner. Not me. You got yourself here, which means you're the only one who can pull yourself out.

That's not a curse, that's freedom.

Look around, your body, your bank account, your mindset, your circle, it's all a reflection of your standards. You can't out-manifest the shit you tolerate. You can't whine your way into progress. You can't hashtag your way into success.

If that stings, good. It means the truth landed where it needed to.

You don't need balance. You don't need motivation. You need standards and follow-through. When the alarm goes off, get up. When it's inconvenient, do it anyway. When your brain starts whispering all the reasons to quit, tell it to shut the fuck up and keep moving. That's how you build trust with yourself again, through repetition, not inspiration.

You want to know what's broken? It's not your luck. It's not your childhood. It's not the economy. It's just you. You've been feeding comfort like it's a reward instead of realizing it's the poison that keeps you stuck.

So here's what happens next: you close this book and go do something about it. Not tomorrow. Not Monday. Now. Clean your space. Go for the walk. Make the call. Handle the thing you've been avoiding. Prove to yourself that you mean it this time.

Stop waiting for the right mood or moment. You've waited long enough.

So here's the final truth:

You're not broken beyond what you can fix. You're not forever unlucky. You're not permanently stuck.

From here on out, every excuse you make is your, choice. Your choice to stay the same, or to grow the hell up and do something about it.

Own your wins. Own your losses. Own your words, your habits, your effort, and every result that follows.

Own. Your. Sh*t.

Because at the end of the day, after all the pages, all the lessons, all the bullshit stripped away, it's still just you and the mirror.

You're the problem.

Now go fucking fix it.

About The Author

Nick Groves ("G") grew up in New Orleans, Chicago, Columbus, and Cincinnati and now resides once again in Columbus. A former satellite television technician turned aviation performance and air-space coordination professional, he knows what it's like to go from middle class to poverty and fight his way back to solid ground.

At one point, he was forced to decide whether his last five dollars would buy gas, food, or keep his pets fed. Spending years clawing his way back up, a moment of clarity sparked a deeper truth: you don't wait for someone else to fix things; you own your problems, you fix your problems. That insight fueled the writing of *Own Your Sh*t: You're The Problem*.

Nick isn't a millionaire guru or untouchable success-story. He's a normal guy doing normal work, married to his wife, Rachel, raising two dogs (Kiwi, the mini-dachshund, and Ammo, the Texas Heeler) and living by this simple motto: **If I want it, I can get it.** He refuses to compromise on adaptability, resourcefulness, and independence. He wrote this book for the person who's tired of waiting, tired of blaming others, and ready to stop negotiating with themselves.

Humility is his strongest weapon and the pretense is his enemy, he will be the first to admit he's "no more capable and just as much an idiot as anyone else." But he also knows this: normal people win when they stop expecting to be rescued. Nick doesn't want you to believe in him. He wants you to believe in yourself.

Acknowledgments

First, I owe nearly everything to my wife, Rachel. You stood by me through the lowest points of my life. The grumpy diet days, 45-minute outdoor workouts in lightning storms, career changes, and even moving to a new city away from your family. You have my heart till its last beat. Through laughs, through tears, and even horror game jump scares, you are the best part of my life.

To my wonderful mom, Aubrey: Thank you for showing me through your own independence and willingness to learn that there is nothing I can't figure out if I put in the work. You taught me that my own hands are the tools needed to build my life.

To my dad, Bob, you showed me that hard work, adaptability, and perseverance matter. That a step that isn't forward doesn't mean failure, and sometimes even when it is, well, that's just how life goes and there's nothing else to do but keep moving.

To my grandparents, Glen & Judy, for being a constant foundation of support and guidance to fall back on. You were always that place I could escape to when I needed a reset.

And finally, to my siblings, Alex & Austin. Thank you for always keeping me honest and reminding me what matters, even when weeks passed between conversations. I'm proud of the people you've become. Even though we don't say it often, I love you both.

Sources Cited

Cusimano, C., Kim, J., & Wong, J. (2023). Effort versus Results: How People Value Work Outcomes Over Intention. Yale School of Management. Referenced in "You Don't Deserve Shit" regarding participation-trophy culture and outcome-based value systems.

University of Calgary. (2021). Neural Correlates of Chronic Procrastination: Amygdala Overactivation and Prefrontal Weakness. Referenced in "You're Not Waiting, You're Hiding" to explain dopamine reward cycles and biological procrastination patterns.

Deci, E. L., & Ryan, R. M. (1985). Self-Determination Theory and Intrinsic Motivation in Human Behavior. New York: Springer. Referenced in "You Don't Need Balance or Motivation," discussing autonomy, competence, and relatedness as motivation drivers.

Obama, B. (2012). Inside the Obama White House: Decision Fatigue and Simplified Living. Interview with Vanity Fair. Referenced in "Build Systems, Not Vibes" regarding minimizing daily decision fatigue.

Jobs, S. & Zuckerberg, M. (Various interviews). Referenced in "Build Systems, Not Vibes" discussing their uniform clothing habits for conserving focus and reducing unnecessary choices.

Ramsey, D. (2013). The Total Money Makeover: A Proven Plan for Financial Fitness. Nashville: Thomas Nelson. Referenced in "Act Like the Person You Want to Be," discussing debt snowball methods and everyday accountability.

Allen, J. (NFL Case Study). Referenced in "Consistency Is King (and Boring as Hell)" as a real-world example of long-term consistency and grit leading to mastery.

The Shopping Cart Theory. (Internet Social Behavior Test). Referenced in "Quit Wrecking Our Shit with Your Shit" as a cultural litmus test of self-governance and moral behavior when no enforcement exists.

Clapper Platform User Data (2025). Referenced in "Quit Wrecking Our Shit with Your Shit" — Stack 'Em or Scatter 'Em section — describing poll results on public behavior and self-report bias.

Aviation Incident Reports (2025). NTSB and ICAO Preliminary Releases. Referenced in "Your Feelings Don't Get a Vote" during discussion of the 2025 aviation safety narrative and media-driven emotional response to incident clusters.

Before You Go — Leave A Review

If this book punched you in the mouth, woke you up, or called you out on your bullshit, good. That means it did its job.

Now I'm asking for something simple: **Leave a review.**

Your review isn't about boosting my ego or chasing stars. It helps the next person who needs this book find it before they waste another year blaming everyone else. That's how we keep this movement growing, one honest review at a time.

You don't have to write an essay. Just tell the truth. What hit you hardest? What changed for you? What chapter called you out?

If it helped you, say so. If it pissed you off, say that too. Either way, your words matter more than silence.

Head over to the store you bought it from—Amazon, Barnes & Noble, wherever—and drop your honest take. You already own your shit. Now share it.

— Nick "G" Groves

Notes